# Forensic Marketing

# Forensic Marketing

## Optimizing results from marketing communication
## The essential guide

**Gavin Barrett**

**The McGraw-Hill Companies**

**London** · New York · St Louis · San Francisco · Auckland
Bogotá · Caracas · Lisbon · Madrid · Mexico
Milan · Montreal · New Delhi · Panama · Paris · San Juan
São Paulo · Singapore · Sydney · Tokyo · Toronto

Published by
McGraw-Hill Publishing Company
Shoppenhangers Road, Maidenhead, Berkshire, SL6 2QL, England
Telephone: 01628 23432
Fax: 01628 770224

---

**British Library Cataloguing in Publication Data**
Barrett, Gavin
    Forensic marketing: the professional's guide to optimizing
    results from marketing communication
    1. Communication in marketing   2. Marketing research
    3. Advertising   4. Public relations
    I. Title
    658.8

    ISBN 0-07-709346-1

**Library of Congress Cataloging-in-Publication Data**
Barrett, Gavin,
    Forensic marketing: the professional's guide to optimizing
    results from marketing communication / Gavin Barrett.
       p.  cm.
    Includes bibliographical references and index.
    ISBN 0-07-709346-1
    1. Communication in marketing.  2. Marketing research.
    3. Advertising.  4. Public relations.  I. Title.
    HF5415.123.B37   1995
    658.8–dc20                            94-42550
                                             CIP

*McGraw-Hill*

A Division of The *McGraw-Hill* Companies

12345 BL 9876

Typeset by BookEns Limited, Royston, Herts
and printed and bound by Biddles Ltd, Guildford, Surrey.

Printed on permanent paper in compliance with ISO Standard 9706

# Contents

Unless otherwise stated Gavin Barrett is the author of the chapter.

# About the contributors

## Wendy Aldiss

Wendy Aldiss has been involved with the use of the telephone as a sales and marketing tool since 1979. She is a telebusiness consultant, trading as Inbound Outbound, and since 1980 she has successfully championed telebusiness, from being a 'cold canvasser' through to her most recent position as managing director of TML; the telemarketing agency of EuroRSCG, Europe's largest marketing communications group. She was awarded the Institute of Director's Diploma in Company Direction in 1991. She was a founding committee member of AIMS (Association for Information Systems in Marketing and Sales) and of Women in Direct Marketing. Inbound Outbound was a founder member of the DMA (UK).

## John Drewry

John Drewry is a copywriter and entrepreneur with experience below-the-line since the late sixties. He is chairman of John Drewry Associates Ltd, a marketing communications company. His specialism is sales and internal communications, which he has provided for many of the largest organizations in Europe including British Telecom, British Gas, Rank Xerox, Philips, Prudential Assurance, Pitney Bowes, Clerical Medical and the *Daily Telegraph*. In his non-commercial time he is chairman of an educational theatre charity in Kent.

## Jim Hodgkins

Jim Hodgkins is an associate director at CCN Marketing, Europe's largest supplier of target marketing services. He is responsible for clients' applications of geodemographic data in their direct marketing campaigns and heads the list services division. He graduated in geography from Manchester University, where he was first involved in the analysis of census data. He has a diploma in direct marketing and speaks at conferences on the applications of geodemographic data.

## Peter Hutton

Peter Hutton is a director of MORI and has been undertaking research since the mid-seventies. He is a graduate in social and political sciences from Cambridge University. His book, *Survey Research for Managers*, was published by Macmillan in 1988.

## Jeffrey Lyes

Jeffrey Lyes is chairman of Good Relations, the public relations consultancy of Lowe Bell Communications Group. He has advised a wide range of companies and organizations—both private and public sector—with leading consultancies since the mid-seventies. A qualified journalist, he cut his teeth in public relations working for the police.

## Wally Olins

Wally Olins is chairman and co-founder of Wolff Olins, one of the world's leading consultancies in corporate identity. He is visiting professor at Lancaster University, UK, and Copenhagen Business School and teaches at leading business schools throughout the world. He is author of a number of books on corporate identity and related matters. His latest book *Corporate Identity* is published by Thames & Hudson in the UK (1988) and Harvard Business School Press in the US (1989). There are also German, French, Spanish and Dutch language editions.

## Stewart Pearson

Stewart Pearson is a leader and innovator in data-based marketing, in particular to add value to major brands. A statistician and economist, his career developed with *Reader's Digest*, O&M Direct and his agency Pearson–Paul–Haworth–Nolan (PPHN). He has launched a new business, ADAMAS Partners, to work with organizations to add value and deliver measurable gains, by creating new relationship marketing programmes.

## Monica E. Seeley

Monica E. Seeley has been an international management

consultant since the late seventies. She specializes in helping organizations, and especially sales and marketing functions to use information technology to gain business benefits. Currently she is conducting an extensive longitudinal research study into why and how senior executives are using information technology to improve their personal effectiveness as executives.

## Richard Webber

Richard Webber is the managing director of CCN Marketing, having joined CCN in 1986 from CACI Marketing Analysis Division where he was vice president and manager, European market analysis operations. He has been involved in the use of census statistics for targeting since 1982 and was one of the early pioneers in the development of the geodemographics industry in the UK. Since joining CCN he has been responsible for the development of CCN's target marketing services, more specifically MOSAIC, customer classification systems and database marketing.

## Robin Wight

Robin Wight began his career in advertising in an unusual way. As an undergraduate at Cambridge, he set up Britain's first student advertising agency. His career went on from there: at the age of 23 he took over from Charles Saatchi as creative director of Richard Cope & Partners. In 1979 he helped start Wight–Collins–Rutherford–Scott (WCRS). In the mid-nineties WCRS is the European flagship of the EuroRSCG group, who are No 1 in Europe and seventh largest in the world. He has served as a marketing adviser to a minister for agriculture, stood as a Conservative candidate for Parliament, and is currently working closely with the Duke of Edinburgh's Award on their Charter for Business.

## Robert M. Worcester

Robert M. Worcester is chairman of MORI (Market & Opinion Research International), which he set up in 1969. He is co-editor of several books including the *Consumer Market Research Handbook* (published in 1986 by McGraw-Hill). He has been an honorary visiting professor in the Graduate Centre for Journalism at City University, London, since 1989, and visiting professor of government at the London School of Economics and Political Science (LSE) since 1992.

# Foreword

### Raoul Pinnell, formerly Director of Marketing, National Westminster Bank

Many of us are constantly striving to gain a deeper understanding of the needs and motivations of today's customers. However, too often we either drown in the data, or end up with limited insights from which we can build differentiated propositions. And our struggle is in the context of an increasing rate in the pace of change. The urgency and responsibility of managers to create a 'future focus' for the businesses has never been more pressing. Does this mean that we have to learn to create a better blend between the analysis of statistical data, and instinctive and intuitive opinions, to create scenario predictions for tomorrow? And if so, how easy is this to do in the hurly-burly of active business life?

We are constantly on the receiving end of a wide variety of opinions and views from people with their own vested interests—unelected consumerists and activists who may not represent 'real opinion'; media sensationalism that dramatizes the problems of our society, but is incapable of offering any inspiring answers. How can we really serve rather than appease? How do we open up large organizations to the realization that we exist only because of, and for, customers?

How does one make sense of all this and get a deep understanding of:

1 what customers value?
2 using this knowledge as the foundation for all of our business actions?
3 going beyond the hype to make it happen?

In the mid-eighties I had the joy of being responsible for introducing a new product range called Findus Lean Cuisine. At the time it received all sorts of accolades from many quarters. My team and I were applauded and credited with a 'marketing breakthrough'. Some assumed that we had found some new 'magic marketing gold-dust'. What was the secret? Time and again I responded with my belief: 'The product tastes good. And I eat it at home'. The product used good ingredients, real food—in an imaginative way. And perhaps it was presented to meet the mood of the times. At that time marketers had got themselves into a mind-set of: 'the product ingredients don't matter—but the product packaging design does'. Somehow they could sleep at night with the notion 'customers are prepared to accept my product—but I certainly wouldn't eat it myself'. That type of cynical attitude never created new sustainable products that touch customers.

However, are personal views and intuition enough? No. We also need a focus on facts. We also need cold objectivity. And this is where I find the observations from academics can be powerful. They do view things from afar. They can see patterns from a different territory. They stop us from looking inwards and indulging in corporate chest-beating. But how do we connect the observations of academics, with the discipline of a focus on data and measuring our results, with our intuition? How do we translate the value of provocation in meaningful ways to those at the front of our businesses who touch customers?

Shopkeepers open their shops daily (or increasingly never close them). How do they learn to keep experimenting and evaluating how to entice more customers to come to their outlet, rather than a similar one down the road? How do we help marketers who listen to the market, who hear the issues, to engage the thousands of staff in large businesses and to deliver the changes to the products and services that customers want? I think we do it through listening and learning from real experience. And using what is relevant. Discarding what is not. Adding to our own store of learning. Filling the vacuum in direction by recognizing the power of our own leadership.

I love this book. I took it in bite-sized chunks—I read chapters on trains, planes, and on the underground. It gave me digestible pieces of—pauses for reflection.

I hope you get value from it too.

# Acknowledgements

Besides my indebtedness to the authors of Chapters 4–12, there are many others to whom I am grateful for advice, ideas and encouragement offered during the book's development, in particular my colleagues at Sundridge Park, John Chadwick, Philip Foster, Peter Herriott, John Alderson, John Mills, Gordon Webster, John van Maurik, David Hickling and Peter Ranft. The support of Julia Scott and the team at McGraw-Hill, both in the UK and USA, has been splendid. Many of the ideas were born out of conversations and problem-solving sessions with clients in all corners of the globe: to them I offer thanks for their insights and challenges. Finally my thanks to Jenny Wessendorff for keeping me to the timetable and to my wife, Sue, for the support and forbearance that creating such a book demands.

# Introduction: why FORENSIC?

The word Forensic has strong overtones of serious crime and its aftermath. For readers whose minds are already filled with images of green-clad boffins wielding blood-stained scalpels and dispassionately discussing the contents of the victim's stomach, let me reassure you and say that the only parallels between the forensic sciences, practised with consummate skill by police laboratories throughout the world, and the subject matter of this book can be found in the fundamental approach to discovering what happened in the past and why.

Some might argue that many crimes are committed in the name of marketing and it might, indeed, be a good idea to get some of the guilty parties in the dock for the general good. Certainly some aspects of marketing bear little scrutiny, notably the persistent levels of self-indulgence and assumptive behaviour.

FORENSIC is a mnemonic (see Fig. I.1) which is examined in detail in Chapter 3. At this initial stage it serves to concentrate the mind on the fundamentals of the marketer's life, which I shall argue should be based rather more on methodical, rational processes, even a scientific approach, than the intuitive art that it has so often come to mean. In the real world of forensic science the watchword is objective evidence leading to the truth—not in itself a bad nostrum for the marketer. Mnemonics, however, are no substitute for developing one's own path to a disciplined approach. While some readers will find the mnemonic checklist helpful as a work tool, for others it will serve better as a pointer towards the shaping of their attitude to marketing. Indeed I intend that the forensic theme be 90 per cent focused on aiding the reader's attitudinal shift and 10 per cent as a direct basis for subsequent marketing process control. It mainly serves the purpose of giving a start-point to the central issue of the book—that the marketing mind-set is ripe for a rethink.

FOCUS on facts
OBSERVATION
RESEARCH
EVALUATION
NEGATIVE indicators
STRATEGY compliance
INERTIAL barriers/factors
CHECK and re-check

**Figure I.1** The FORENSIC model

Besides the centrality of the forensic approach to marketing, and, in particular, to the deployment of the communications tool-set, I shall explore the positional dilemmas for facing marketers: getting the professional approach sufficiently right to allow successful relationships with the internal corporate market (especially at senior levels), the supply-side with their diverse offerings and, of course, the market-place. This positional force-field is largely instrumental in leading marketers astray: satisfying one polarity is almost always at the expense of another.

What I hope the book will reveal is how to develop approaches to the various elements of marketing that will allow all professionals to have their cake and eat it. If it were not a politically discredited expression I should talk at length about the need for a back to basics approach, stripping away the barnacle-like accretions that marketing has acquired since the forties, and which obscure the obvious and evidently marketable proposition that it is the identification of mutual stakeholder advantage that is, or ought to be, at the heart of all business purpose.

Figure I.2 demonstrates the interaction between these stakeholders and the points where forensic approaches will make the difference between the ordinary solution and the exceptional. Securing ownership of this particular value-system is the overall purpose of Forensic Marketing.

I am indebted to the distinguished authors of Chapters 4–12. They are giants in their respective fields of marketing communications. Their given mandate was to champion their element of the communications mix without compromise to the others. In so doing they strip away many myths and legends and, in their place, make powerful and persuasive cases for why their particular approach is appropriate in specific circumstances. Without this expert advocacy of what are already complex ideas, I do not believe it would be

**Figure I.2** Applying the FORENSIC model to the decision-making processes of the marketing function

possible to achieve the aim of the book—an objective understanding of choice for the marketing professional and the other key stakeholders in the discipline.

Gavin Barrett
Sundridge Park

# 1

# The devil and the deep blue sea

This book is about choice and high-risk choice in particular. Marketing is primarily concerned with the management of choice. This would be challenging enough if it were simply a matter of customers having choice of use for disposable income, or commercial buyers for solutions to their needs, but it is not. The ways in which marketing professionals manage that choice are bewildering in their complexity, reflecting the range of demands placed upon the marketing function, from development of strategic markets to tactical opportunism in the 'fourth quarter fire fight'—when the race to achieve the sales budget becomes intense, and, not unusually, irrational.

Rosemary Stewart (1982) puts choice in context in her revealing study of what managers and professionals actually do. Her analysis demonstrates that all of us are faced with demands, constraints and choices. Demands are the largely non-negotiable component—targets, budgets, deadlines, decisions and actions. Constraints are the ever present factors of time, money and people, coupled with rules, protocols, standards of conformity and personal limitations in terms of attitudes, knowledge and skills to deal with the demands. Choices are about courses of action open to us in meeting the demands placed upon us. The less we know, the less choice we have. This is as true of the customer as it is of the manager.

Given that marketing professionals will want to satisfy as much market demand as can be secured profitably, they will need to be well informed about the choices available for the task. The constraints that they labour under vary enormously, but near the top of the list will be found budgets and risk aversion—typically quite closely related. In the following chapters we shall look at the demands, constraints and choices facing the marketing function and those whose roles require them to think marketing. In so doing we shall examine the various orientations of marketers, from ego-driven enthusiasts to the rigorously analytical, and see what the dilemmas really are. Then we shall review the orthodox thinking about marketing strategy, with the various theories competing for share of mind, and how political reality usually comes out on top.

The greater part of the book deals with what marketers can do with their disposable budget to achieve the aims of their strategy. Besides being the fun part of the role, it is the area of greatest choice and maximum confusion. Never in the realms of business have so few had so much to play with to such devastating effect— devastating to profitability as well as, more rarely, enduring success.

This kaleidoscope of choice, stimulant and risk is what the marketer must manage and manage consistently in full knowledge of what the choices really are, how they can be sorted and how the decisions made can be evaluated for their effectiveness. It is often argued that no one actually wants choice, they want confidence in their decision process. Forensic Marketing is aimed at those who want to grow their confident application of the communications tool-set. This is to an extent where even the rigour of forensic analysis of the scene of their 'crimes' will show the discerning mind of a professional at work, rather than the transient enthusiasm of the amateur.

## The quart from the pint pot

There is, of course, never enough budget to do everything that we want. Even if there was at the start of the year, by the time the need for a final big push to finish the year in fine style is recognized by the whole management team, the cupboard is bare. We often feel that we are the victim of circumstances rather than the maker of them. Sales revenue below plan, general belt-tightening to reduce costs, product launch delays, service levels below standard and a rich palette of acts of God in the form of government waywardness, foreign exchange markets, unseasonable weather and the latest oriental 'flu, all conspire to sabotage the elegance of the marketing plan, written, of course, in sobriety as part of the annual budget-setting round.

Besides budgetary constraints, the marketer has to live with the variable nature of management policy—a very flexible friend or foe. Few marketers would deny the need for a consistent strategy for marketing in all its manifestations, whether brand development, service quality, product development, customer retention, distribution or profitability growth. The paradigm seldom allows this. Tactical expedience and management whim ensure that demand or enthusiasm for today's results will generally triumph over strategic reason. The very same arguments colour the column inches of debate on short-termism and lack of investment in manufacturing infrastructure that have dominated the media in the USA and UK since the early eighties.

The absence of consistent approaches to strategy formulation and implementation produces high levels of waste, missed opportunities and substitutional effect, rather than incremental gain. At its most flagrant, the tactical use of price-led sales promotion, while committed to building a durable value-for-money platform, amounts to criminal negligence of strategy in sectors where price has been shown to be creating a commodity market. A notable example of this relentless pursuit of the tactical option has been the personal computer (PC) market on a global scale: practitioners know that it is an unsustainable policy. Even those producers who have managed to take cost down ahead of price have reducing margin left for investment in brand values that will be needed when cost productivity can yield no more. They know it. We all know it. Yet this group hysteria continues: no one will get off the tumbrel as it races to the place of execution.

Expectations of what marketing can achieve may be unrealistic among management colleagues. What marketing does or ought to do is seldom clear to management teams, hence the belief in the white magic of the agency world. This implied belief in the total resilience of marketing strategy to any form of tactical distortion has been allowed to happen—allowed by marketers, perhaps none too clear about the issues themselves. What is it that stops marketing professionals from formulating and consistently delivering strategic marketing? The answer is something that we shall address in this book, but as a clue we might consider the siren call of the supply-side with its constant innovation of new and arguably improved techniques for reaching those parts of the market that other tools cannot. To resist these blandishments outside, and the insidious effect they may have on less well-informed management colleagues within, requires the self-control of a saint to resist, let alone critically evaluate.

If marketers are tested in the fire managing the internal market, they know the temptations of the devil when it comes to selecting their communications tool-set. This dilemma state is, we might argue, the result of generations of tolerance of intuitive approaches to the marketing role and a sustained failure to adopt a more rationalist, analytical, even forensic critical faculty. Faith, hope and charity are virtues—in the right place. In marketing? Surely not.

The trouble may be that marketers have a fondness for the intuitive over the reasoned since it supports the theory that marketing is an art not a science. It is a perfectly natural viewpoint, given that so much else in management is fuelled by an experimental approach. Where it falls down is in the field of learning from experience. Too often the intuitive marketer cannot articulate why a particular campaign is working or why not. If that cannot be done, how then can wisdom be found?

If the devil is the voice of ego-driven leaping in the dark, then the deep blue sea is the difficulty of rational analysis of experience.

## What are the prizes beyond this awesome choice?

Marketers are all looking, as Nigel Piercy (1991) of Cardiff Business School argues in his important text, *Market-led strategic change*, for 'new practical tools for evaluating the marketing performance of their organizations and, as a result of that evaluation, for identifying how best to improve marketing performance'. He goes on to argue that 'the most common reasons why marketing fails in practice ... are to do with muddled and confused management decisions about strategic marketing issues and a lack of real commitment where it counts most to making marketing work'.

This just criticism of management commitment is echoed by Michael Porter (1985) in his authoritative *Competitive advantage*: 'the failure of many firms' strategies stems from an inability to translate a broad competitive strategy into the specific action steps required to gain competitive advantage' (page *xv*). We start to see that marketing may be caught on the horns of a dilemma that recognizes what ought to be done, but is unable to deliver because the specific actions are not valued in the management ethos. Paying lip-service to best practice in marketing is hardly a first in the pantheon of cultural tokenism. We might just as easily look at contemporary ideas of empowerment, collegiate behaviour, multiple careers, upward appraisal and women in management to find equal examples of yes meaning maybe and certainly not now.

We shall examine why this gap exists between what good

marketing is thought to be and what actually happens. Central to the debate is the view that marketing may be overprotected from the searching analysis commonly afforded to other forms of investment, and its partner in misery, the sales function. What, we must ask, are the things that marketing ought to be valued for and, by the same token, be measured upon?

We could start with a shortlist of goals for marketing that, if delivered, might change the ways in which it is evaluated and, therefore, esteemed. Marketing is not as authoritative in management debate as it might be. This list could alter that perception:

- Improvement in business results
- Measurable results
- Evidence of value for money from the supply-side
- Consistency of application within the strategic framework
- Management credibility
- Accommodation of ego-driven management decisions
- Learning from experience.

Briefly explored, each of these headings reveals surprising gaps between the vaunted claims and the reality.

## Improvement in business results

General managers are targeted to achieve the two virtues of cost and revenue productivity, within a risk management framework. Cost productivity means eliminating the cost of what you cannot measure and leveraging the effectiveness of any cost that you can measure but cannot do without. It is not a concept for the sentimental. Revenue productivity is, at least in theory, another hard measure concept—sales by channel by product, return on sales, sales per employee, cash flow, stock turn and so on. In reality it is often larded with sentiment, myths and legends. But then it is the sales community's role to create optimism and belief that water can be pushed up hill, as long as it is left to them.

Both concepts are, in themselves, virtuous but commonly misapplied, especially in the marketing functional area. If the organization has no clear view as to what improvements in performance it could achieve, how then can it manage its affairs in such a way as those improvements are made? How many organizations know what marketing could do for them, let alone what they presently deliver? Not many.

Similarly, how many organizations know the cost productivity of the various tools of marketing and their impact on the performance of the business? Again, none too many. The oft-quoted saying of, variously, Lord Leverhulme, Henry Ford, and others, that 'I know that half my advertising works, but I only wish I knew which half', is too true to be funny. Why do we not know which half works?

The dilemma for marketers is that strategic marketing is validated only in hindsight, whereas decisions on marketing spend need to be made with foresight. Given the choice, most of us would be tempted to err on the side of caution and go for easy results rather than quality of strategy: after all we might not be around to collect the prize.

That temptation would be wrong. Sustainable growth comes from the courage to do more of those things that bring results than our competitors do. Whether those things are tactical or, better still, strategic investments, they need to be done in as well informed a way as is possible. This concept demands that the evidential link between action and reaction is positively established: that applies to marketing too.

It is often surprising to find how unclear managements are about the things they think they can improve; certainly they know about costs on the whole, but they can be remarkably unsure as to the proactive investment options available to them. In later chapters we shall look at some of the major choices available to the marketer and how they can be exercised through well-informed decisions.

## Measurable results

Shortly after the privatization process of the water industry in the UK was completed, one company's finance director was minded to challenge the value of nearly £1 million expenditure on public relations (PR). 'Show me the return on this investment and you can have the budget'. Hands thrown up in horror, a search for the witches in *Macbeth* to conjure some dire fate for the hapless challenger, and a pessimistic view that while PR was obviously a good thing to have, its benefit could not be shown. On closer examination the PR department were able to identify some thirty commercial performance measures that were directly linked to their activity, the most notable being the impact on debtor days of a well-informed customer base who had a full understanding of what investment was being made in infrastructure, what was being done to beat sea pollution and why hose-pipe bans were the right policy.

The correlation between attitude surveys and debtor days improvement was absolute and credible to the finance director. The budget was confirmed.

The marketing professionals were, arguably, more surprised than their challenger. The received wisdom was that PR is not accountable, merely essential. It took three days of hard persuasion to shift the orientation from one of 'It cannot be done' to 'Do you think thirty ratios is rather pushing our luck?' A paradigm shift.

If it can be shown that spend on PR is directly related to business results then how much more advantage would come from demonstrating the business effectiveness of the full communications tool-set? If results are the most valued cultural symbol in business then it seems a wise investment of time to demonstrate the clear accountability of the function so that its authority is developed.

## Evidence of value for money from the supply-side

A senior City of London lawyer remarked during the early recovery stage (mid 1993) from the UK recession that 'our clients are becoming too wise. If they go on learning at this rate about what we really can do, they will see our fees as exaggerated and avoidable. We are not worth what we used to be; the market will not stand it'. The result has been a sharp decline in real achieved fee rates by all branches of the legal profession.

It takes a sophisticated buyer to cope with a sophisticated solution. It is equally true that a sophisticated buyer will know when the solution is not. If the financial services markets in Europe and the USA continue to develop buyer sophistication at their present rate, the role of the intermediary is doomed. Already in the USA, most large corporate organizations can raise capital more cheaply than their bankers—partly a function of credit worthiness of course, but equally they know how to do it and what matters. The UK's most successful retail bank has become Marks and Spencer. The UK's most successful corporate banker for several of the last few years has been BP. The poacher has turned gamekeeper and knows when it is being sold less than full measure.

The question stands, how sophisticated are marketers in evaluating the value-for-money of their suppliers' offerings? The answer, like the curate's egg, is good in parts. We shall see, however, that for large proportions of the marketing spend, the accountability factor is low. Above-the-line advertising is commonly cited as unquantifiable in its benefits. Telemarketing is seen as very quantifiable. The evidence that this is important to clients comes from the USA where expenditure on the (quantifiable) techniques of telemarketing and selling exceeds press and TV advertising combined. The writing is on the wall—marketers must establish the accountable performance of each of the tools and techniques we deploy.

## Consistency of application within the strategic framework

Joseph Stalin made the management mistake of believing that whatever went into his five-year plans would happen. It is written, therefore it is so. History mercifully makes a mockery of such dogma. The lesson ought to be well learned that a business strategy that is not dynamic, adaptable and consistently applied is likely to drive the business on to the rocks. Conformity with a single set of values and beliefs at a moment of history is a remarkably shaky basis for future development. Yet marketing strategy and its elder associate, business strategy, too often have a dogmatic tone, demanding slavish conformity rather than elasticity and consistency.

If conformity is blind, the absence of any strategic clarity is worse. We shall examine in the next chapter what marketers must demand of the business strategy, if only to establish where magnetic north is, then everyone in the organization can be issued with a compass.

Marketing has a major role in surveying the past, present and future within the strategy formulation process. It is the trustee of the learning from experience that will help the organization avoid the pitfalls of unproductive repetition of mistakes. It is the champion of the customer within the citadel and must identify their future needs and articulate them in terms of deliverable solutions.

If marketing has this important contribution to make, why then does it allow the customer to be marginalized during the implementation phase? Arguably the correlation between enhancing shareholder value and customer satisfaction is still sufficiently under-developed in the mind of general managers that the wisdom of vesting tactical authority for business strategy implementation in the marketing function, to ensure consistency, has not yet been established as widely as it ought. There are, of course, notable examples of marketing-led organizations such as Procter and Gamble, Nestlé, Coca Cola, Disney and Sainsbury, but even in an example like Virgin Atlantic the championship of customer satisfaction came at the cost of being able to satisfy shareholders and led to Richard Branson's decision to take the group private again.

## Management credibility

How credible is the marketing function in your organization? If it is high what has led to it? If not, then why not?

Just as brand values have to be earned, so does confidence in marketing by general managers. Of the functional areas in business, marketing is the least trusted. Its accountability is so far under-developed that it might be argued that the most effective job marketing has done is to conceal the fact that it is an emperor with no clothes.

It is difficult to establish authority over the customer impacting parts of the business without high levels of internal credibility. This is certainly true if lip-service to customer satisfaction is to be converted into real levels of customer focus and delivery. The credibility that marketers must acquire consists of being able to demonstrate the value of what we do, not what we say. The forensic approach is about evidence, in hard fact terms, though the historical caution of 'anything you say will be written down and may be given in evidence' applies in full measure in some politically driven organizations.

The enthusiasm for Hammer and Champy's (1993) radical text on *Re-engineering the corporation* of many business leaders in the USA and UK suggests that a number are tired of the barnacle-like accretions of custom and practice that have grown up in organizations and have concluded that Michael Porter's (1985) 'Value-Chain' (pages 33–63) has become clogged with myths and legends about the value of this or that function. They are demanding that the fundamentals of business processes are assessed and the added value of each is demonstrable and evidential.

Marketers are not immune from the rigour of this re-engineering mind-set and have much to offer it. We all need to be sure that we know where we fit in the value-chain and where we provide real leverage to the key business processes. When that linkage is clear, marketing will have come of age.

## Accommodation of ego-driven management decisions

Happily for most of us, management teams are still built of people, not expert computer systems. They have their human frailties just as marketers do. They come armed with prejudices, experiences, lacunae and fears not dissimilar to our own. They can feel as we do and identify with our hopes and aspirations. They can be persuaded of our viewpoint.

Equally they can be as deaf and as blind as our worst nightmares portray, pursuing competitive vendettas, chasing phantasmagorical opportunities, acquiring Star Wars technology to shoot turkeys, and selective in their mania from one day to the next.

That is what makes management interesting and challenging to the rationalist marketer who would rather some semblance of logic informed decisions than none at all. What seems to characterize poor management decisions overall is a high assumptiveness content—a belief in self-generated propaganda and self-image, rather than objective evaluation of the facts. We might ask why that is so. Not the least of the possibilities is that facts are hard to come by in terms of marketing and future direction.

Great entrepreneurs have not waited around for their marketing professionals to do an in-depth report and risk analysis. They have a powerful intuitive feel for opportunities that their experience has confirmed positively on enough occasions for it to become the established truth. How many entrepreneurs have got it right for a while and then lost it, because their vision of the right order of things has failed to encompass shifts in the market and competitive reactions to the original act of genius? Sir Clive Sinclair would not be the man he is had he not defied the wisdom of the age and sought to popularize the computer with his seminal ZX80 and derivatives. The magisterial success he attained in this field was not achieved with the ill-starred C5 electric car. Had he access to quality market intelligence or did he ignore it? Perhaps we shall never know, but the lesson for marketers is that powerful intuitive drive among business leaders is perfectly OK if it can be consolidated with quality market analysis.

Striking the right relationship with the ego factor in business is a challenge that is not going to go away. What may improve the balance between ego and rationality, or the art and science of management, is that the latter qualities come from a willingness to subject decisions to evaluation and learning. In many years of monitoring marketing and business successes I have not found too much evidence of this partnership of ideas. But it is coming and fast. Hence this book.

## Learning from experience

The direct-marketing industry has come of age. It is now acceptable to talk of laser-precision marketing, regression analysis, Latin Squares, interactive campaigns and so on. Yet these are relatively recent phenomena on the wide stage of international marketing. Until the eighties the sophisticated tools of the direct-marketing world were administered in private by consenting adults in the *Reader's Digest* organization or *Time-Life*. What they knew, and the rest of us did not, was that the behaviour of markets could be modelled provided that there was a relentless search for behavioural data on as large a scale as possible. *Reader's Digest* is the epitome of how to accumulate data over decades and use it to refine a process engine capable of extraordinary feats of prediction.

Central to these core values is the willingness to learn from each and every experience. Today, the direct-marketing industry makes adequate use of testing, with no one solution being backed alone. Of course, the use of direct mail or telemarketing allows for high degrees of measurement and correlation, with single variables in the marketing mix being tested one at a time. That is quite proper to the particular channel of direct marketing.

However, we should continue to ask ourselves just how much we learn from other forms of marketing, and do so with high levels of objectivity, rather than the selective use of results to confirm a prejudice or belief? Generally, learning from experience is low where the organizational culture is intolerant of error. Imagine being challenged on why you are mounting any form of tests at all: 'Don't you know the right answer—what am I paying you for?' Blame cultures do not want risk. They are prone to driving looking in the rear-view mirror: the past is always so much more attractive. Consequently they do not want new discovery or the risk entailed in making it.

On the other hand, a tolerant forgiveness culture puts a high premium on learning from experience. Watching a rehearsal of the choir of King's College, Cambridge (arguably the greatest choir anywhere) I was struck by the occasional hand going up, whether from boy chorister or experienced lay clerks, while the performance continued uninterrupted. Only if the same hand at the same point in the music went up did the director of music stop and offer help. Each chorister was signalling the first time that he had made an error and knew it, and the second time, more rarely, that he could not overcome the difficulty. It is easy to see why it is the leading choir. A total forgiveness culture, self-aware, seeking the highest standards and demanding to learn from its experience. Would that were an easily transferable orientation.

Marketers should set out deliberately to test the frontiers of experience and to challenge the received wisdom. Only then will we know whether we actually hit the bull's eye or just the edge of the target.

## The overwhelming case for a marketing strategy

This chapter has sought to offer more dilemmas than answers. The status quo is to be challenged. But a point comes when looking into the abyss induces vertigo and the inclination to go on and make the leap with one's hang-glider loses its attraction.

Yes, we are often between the devil and the deep blue sea and too often it is our fault. Marketing is not as credible as it ought to be; it is less valued in the councils of management than say the finance or operations functions. With few exceptions the marketing strategy represents an idealized view of the world rather than the harsh and manageable reality.

What is needed is a process that provides sufficient clarity of vision, with commercial integrity that the implementation of the marketing strategy is seen as management's highest priority. Marketers make their own luck and that of their business.

# 2

# If you don't know where you are going, you will end up somewhere else

In Chapter 1 we considered the proposition that marketers would do well to increase their accountability and perceived credibility by providing more tangible evidence of the outputs of marketing activity, and in such ways as will establish the clear correlative link with accepted business performance indicators. This challenge applies equally to professional suppliers to the marketing function. As buyer sophistication grows so does the need to demonstrate significant added value. Mystique and technical jargon are poor substitutes for proof.

The well-informed marketer, learning from structured and imaginative experiences, is a mandatory orientation for all who aspire to formulate marketing strategy, let alone implement it. Without this analytical orientation, the lessons of the past will not be learned and a firm basis for new experimentation not established. Well-informed marketing is concerned to achieve sufficiency of risk in competitive terms, without the unnecessary risks of repeating old errors, one's own or someone else's. Sustainable competitive advantage comes from being more often right than wrong, in strategic and tactical terms, than competitors. It does not require marketers to be any more visionary than anyone else, rather they should be capable of asking the right questions.

The best strategies have at their core a relentless search for durable streams of customer needs unfettered by contemporary allegiances to products and markets. They put a high premium on consistent application of brand values that grow both in magnetic pull and market leadership. I use brand values here to denote the general perceptions of customers rather than a more specific definition.

In this chapter we shall review the processes of marketing strategy formulation and the key questions that need to be put. Here again, there are too many choices, too many models and matrices designed to take us in the right direction. The well-informed marketer will start with a set of fundamental tests and use further techniques only to refine the strategic statements.

## Why bother with a marketing strategy at all?

Marketing strategy is the prime expression of the business strategy. It is the means whereby the objectives of the business, both long and short term, will be delivered. At the most prosaic level it is a means of ensuring that there will be any customers around to savour our solutions—creating our future markets as well as finding them. It is also concerned to ensure that our organization is well placed for the competitive fray, with the resources and focus to optimize the opportunities along the way. Above all, the marketing strategy exists to mark the boundaries, to provide a bench-mark fit for all new initiatives and to minimize internal polarization. If the latter is tolerated, there is only one certain winner, our competitors.

The Delphi technique (named after the Oracle of Delphi in classical Greek mythology) of future prediction suggests that if a number of people are asked to nominate three or four key factors likely to have a major influence on the business outlook, they will come up with a couple upon which they are all agreed, albeit independently arrived at. This aggregation of intuitive beliefs is important because it provides one basis for agreement on future direction, in the absence of more rational bases. These intuitive beliefs will, of course, reflect prejudices, desires, hopes and a need for some longer-term certainty, however spurious. It is this need to create our futures that makes the strategic process possible, since a purely rational application of logic to the future would be difficult and probably unrewarding. We might say of the future 'If we can dream it, we can do it!'

Most strategic commentators warn that the future is rushing towards us. It is not an option to maintain the status quo, guarding the gains of the past and, like the proverbial French peasant, keeping the gold under the mattress. Competitors have a powerful interest in taking our gains away and, if they are successful, it means that by definition we are in a worse condition. Strategy is there to give purpose, focus and direction to Darwinian competitive drive. We ignore the need for continuous proactive investment in our future at great peril. This was a lesson learned the hard way by IBM which,

Canute-like, sought to resist competitive onslaught with internal denial of even the possibility of their success. Complacency took a heavy toll in head-count terms and it is clear today that IBM has resolved never again to allow overwhelming self-belief to blind it to the harsh reality of global competition.

If, therefore, there is only the future to aim for, what should the strategist consider?

## SWOT or something deeper?

Figure 2.1 shows a simplified approach to strategic planning, used by many organizations to start the process. Most of the stages of this model are already well understood and explored in depth elsewhere, so I shall here concentrate on those aspects that will, in the ultimate, have the greatest bearing on marketing and marketing communications.

A significant proportion of strategic reviews fall at the first fence by failing to establish the full gamut of stakeholder expectations. These stakeholders are the various publics that we shall meet again later in the field of PR: customers, shareholders, employees, suppliers, regulators, public, government, competitors, prospective customers and shareholders and generations as yet unborn. As Shakespeare's Cassius puts it in *Julius Caesar* (Act III, sc. i)

How many ages hence
Shall this our lofty scene be acted over
In states unborn and accents yet unknown!

It is with the eyes of future stakeholders, as well as those of the present, that we must evolve our strategy.

While some stakeholder expectations are reasonably predictable—shareholder need for sustainable economic value added, for example—others are more elusive—suppliers' and customers' to name but two. With the rising enthusiasm for supplier partnerships, sharing in joint strategic developments, their inclusion in the process seems less remarkable than once it did. Many organizations will not have the resources alone to meet competition head on; the alliance with key suppliers leverages their combined weight by an order of magnitude.

Customers as stakeholders have featured in the literature for some decades, but it is far from clear as to whether this is tokenism or not. I express serious doubt, if only because of the seemingly born-again

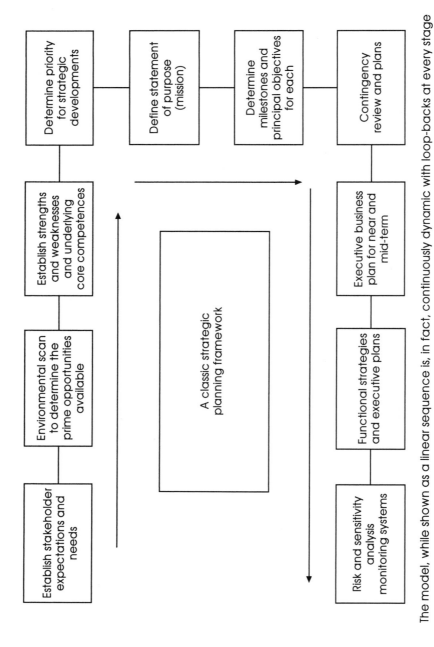

The model, while shown as a linear sequence is, in fact, continuously dynamic with loop-backs at every stage

**Figure 2.1** A classic strategic planning framework

realization among some organizations that perhaps something ought to be done about customer retention, rather than replacement. In spite of well-attested evidence (McKenna, 1992) that it is far easier to sell to existing customers than to win new ones, the disposable customer remains a generic fact of life (or corporate death). Yet without customers the whole strategic intent is valueless.

The customer stakeholder in strategy formulation can provide vital inputs:

- Brand perceptions
- Buying motivations
- Competitive awareness
- Informed evaluation of products and services
- Possible needs
- The size of the credibility gap—ours versus the competition.

All of which helps to establish the start-line for change. Coupled with a rational analysis of customer behaviour over the previous strategic period, it becomes possible to see if customer perceptions today are at variance with recent practice and, if so, in which direction. While markets are often surprisingly conservative in the face of innovation, they seem to have an unerring sense of the possible, and hence should be heeded. Similarly, markets are capable of expressing valuable insights into future needs: the art is to help them articulate their intuitive feelings. We shall return to this theme when considering the role of research techniques.

The most demanding stakeholder grouping, whose views will dominate the strategic process, is corporate management itself: not unreasonably so, but a minefield for the unwary. If the management orientation is fixed upon survival rather than growth, then the past will seem more attractive than the future. They must be challenged: the past was an imperfect place, raddled with age and suffused with snares and delusions. The present may be uncomfortable and frustrating, as it is, by definition, reality. The only direction worth taking is forward, and forward with enterprise and commitment. The future holds the means to put right what is wrong today, to apply the lessons of past experiences and to build something of enduring value.

The word growth is misleading in that it implies volume. It does not need to. Rather, it should mean development in capability and enterprise. Key words like resilience, imagination, sufficiency of risk, competitiveness, responsiveness and effectiveness provide opportunities for growth. If the strategy formulation process is not geared to growth in these more specialist senses then it is unlikely to deliver the volumetric definition either.

Senior management will subscribe to this positive, dynamic orientation if they are equipped to see the future in terms that will feel credible and attractive. It is part of the marketing function to demonstrate that a future return for all stakeholders is attainable and realistic. Where marketing needs to put in extraordinary effort is in overcoming too much rationality during the first testing stage of strategy formulation. Marketing must drive up choice and viable options and then facilitate evaluation. Thinking beyond is the ability to imagine the future in terms of the future, uninhibited by present value systems. It is the real basis for bold strategy.

Sadly, the received wisdom of strategy formulation marginalizes this capacity to move out of the cocoon of today through the medium of the SWOT Analysis (see Fig. 2.2). If applied in the conventional way the process requires practitioners to define the business's present Strengths and Weaknesses before addressing its Opportunities and Threats (i.e. SWOT). This guarantees a view of the future firmly rooted in the present or past. While not a disaster for most businesses, this timid approach may well ensure that the business fails to see the major market opportunities of the future, simply because it rejects them on the grounds that it has not got the appropriate strengths. Why this reverse logic should be tolerated the length and breadth of the business community worldwide eludes me.

Arguably, the problem lies in the universal failure to see that the speed of change is accelerating at an unprecedented rate. I argue that today's apparent strengths may turn out to be a millstone about our necks in addressing the potential of the future. The alternative view that I put forward is to concentrate on potential *Opportunities* and their attendant *Threats* and then establish what *Strengths* would (OTSW) be needed to derive the full benefit. A straightforward (inhibiting Weaknesses) comparison between current and desired strengths would establish the first gap to be addressed by the strategy.

An alternative and hugely attractive view comes from two distinguished academics, Gary Hamel and C.K. Prahalad, in their series of articles for the *Harvard Business Review* in the early nineties. In the first, 'The core competences of the organization', Hamel and Prahalad (1991) argue that strategy formulation ought to concentrate on the durable strengths of the organization at a root system

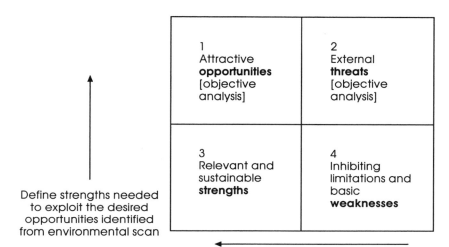

**Figure 2.2** SWOT Analysis in the FORENSIC sequence

level, rather than the more typical SWOT Analysis. They propose that organizations drill down to find the genetic code that allows the core strengths or capabilities to become useful. In testing the capabilities of the organization Hamel and Prahalad apply three beguilingly easy tests that, in the aggregate, prove tantalizingly elusive.

The tests of core capability are as follows:

- They provide access to a wide variety of market applications.
- They bring real and significant benefit to customers in their perception.
- They are difficult or impossible to imitate.

Clearly, if all three conditions are satisfied the core competence is powerful indeed. Organizations, in considering their strategic purpose, could do worse than seek to identify their core competences. Once articulated, the core competences become the central focus for management. In applying our own analytical methodology, (work undertaken by Gavin Barrett and John Chadwick of PA Consulting Group's Sundridge Park Management Centre), to establish the Hamel and Prahalad competences of a wide variety of organizations, we have found them to be rare, often under-developed and unrecognized by management (see Table 2.1).

**Table 2.1** A structured approach to core competence

| Phase 1 | Phase 2 | Phase 3 |
|---|---|---|
| Stakeholders' definition of desired future position—The vision statement: where we want to be | What unique assets have we got that underpin the core competences? | What is the role of each individual member of the organization in growing the core competence(s)? |
| SWOT Analysis (sequence: OTSW) Environmental scan Define durable opportunities and strengths needed for them | What factors make them unique? Can we replicate them? Where do they lie within the organization? | Establish that asset management and development is a priority within the normal operations of the organization |
| Isolate the capabilities that lie behind the durable strengths—What must we be able to do and what capabilities will we need? | Which functional areas of the organization can harness our core competences and can enrich them? | Include 'Your contribution to core competence' within the organization's appraisal systems |
| Apply three tests of core competence to the list of capabilities identified Determine the gap between capabilities and core competence status | Define why these core competences are needed and identify other processes that would benefit from developing them | Define training and development needs to support the capacity of individuals and teams to contribute to core competence management |
| List the core competences and develop a management commitment to manage them closely | What are we going to do specifically to maintain and enhance our core competences? | Reprise: where does each core competence fit within the organization's strategy? |

| Develop a priority list to convert latent competences into core competences | What is, or should be, management's role in sustaining and growing core competences? | What is the communications plan to ensure stakeholder ownership of our core competences and their primacy in our strategic plans? |

An abbreviated schematic of the Sundridge Park methodology to help organizations establish and manage their core competences, based on Hamel and Prahalad's (1991) conceptual model. Once established, core competences become the prime focus of senior management and underpin the business and marketing strategies. When firmly established and deployed, core competences deliver massive competitive advantage

In this journey of discovery, however, many management teams have discovered to their horror that almost everything they do is imitable, often without much effort. Bankers have discovered that the only significant differentiator open to them is the transactional history of their customers. Having realized this, a number have observed that it is the interpretation of that transactional data that holds the key to core competence. Data that cannot be converted first into information and then, through structured marketing, into knowledge, are of very limited value.

In service organizations these core competences often centre upon data assets rather than business processes. Whereas manufacturing businesses have some chance to develop unique tools and techniques, possibly open to protection through patent law, the service providers are commonly in a trap of their own making, namely product and price imitation—a strategy that has little future.

Hamel and Prahalad (1990) cite numerous examples to confirm their thesis: Canon as a world-leader in low-level laser applications, Citibank for global trading technologies, and National Panasonic for the integration of computers and communication. Subsequently, for example, we believe that Reuters have core competence in information dissemination, *Reader's Digest* in list management, Prudential Assurance in distribution, Honda in internal combustion engine technology, Sony in miniaturization, and Sheraton Hotels in service delivery.

In a second article, 'Corporate imagination and expeditionary marketing', Hamel and Prahalad (1991) explore these notions, which build upon the earlier core competence model and show how organizations can stake out future territory by creatively exploiting their competences, often through fusion with other competences held by historic competitors. This concept of strategic alliance to achieve unassailable competitive distance ahead of the pack puts a high premium on both the management of core competences and the ability to integrate them imaginatively to create an even more potent cocktail of competitive advantage.

Key to this view of the world is the notion that we must give up thinking in terms of markets and products and, instead, think needs and solutions. They urge us to abjure the habit of viewing the future through eyes blinded by current products and technologies. Through knowing the needs that will dominate the demand-side, and how they may be met through solutions rooted in core competences, organizations are rendered capable of huge advances ahead of their competition.

The marketer needs to go further and see how the core competences of the organization, duly enriched with corporate imagination and lateral thought, can be made sufficiently visible to customers that they increasingly inform the brand values. Clearly if that corporate transformation can be achieved, the marketing strategy is written.

## In the absence of core competences?

They are elusive, rare and well guarded by their owners. So what to do if you have no idea of your business's core competences? Besides the inverted SWOT Analysis reviewed above, there are numerous models to help define the optimum strategic direction and some are worth rehearsing in this introductory chapter, forming, as it does, the backdrop to the successful deployment of the communications tool-set.

Ansoff's Matrix (Ansoff, 1968) is one of the simplest and most approachable (see Fig. 2.3). The choices are simple: more of the same to someone else or something new to someone you know, with every combination in between? Given that it is rare for businesses to maximize their penetration of their home markets, it makes sense to sustain momentum in terms of market support. The

Market options open

| | | |
|---|---|---|
| P r o d u c t | Current range to current markets [penetration] | Current range to new markets [market expansion] |
| O p t i o n s | New range to current markets [development and retention] | New range to new markets [business diversification] |

**Figure 2.3** Ansoff's Matrix

well-informed marketer must quantify this heartland and the relative
share held, as well as evaluating the trend of this share.

Then, the marketer will seek to establish if further markets can be
found for the current product portfolio to release the potential for
economies of scale and hence some price-based competitiveness.
Winning these incremental markets requires judgement as to
whether the yield justifies the investment, particularly if resources
are limited. It may not make sense to divert precious budget into
keeping an old product alive for pursuit of new markets, if that
means that new product development is postponed to a point
where it is no longer possible. Market extensions are often a fatal
trap for the unwary and the inert, and should not be allowed to
mask the harsh realities of market obsolescence. Innovate or die has
a persuasive ring to it.

New product development (NPD) for existing or new markets has
the attraction of forward momentum (see Fig. 2.4). The discipline
involved, eloquently detailed in Malcolm McDonald's (1984) classic
textbook *Marketing plans*, harnesses the full skills of marketers. That
the hit rate for NPD is poor has much to do with assumptiveness—
the triumph of enthusiasm and self-belief over rational evaluation of
markets. The popular music industry represents a blatant example of
hope springing eternal—perhaps a hundred singles released for only
one to achieve any sort of hit parade success. That pop music is a
fashion item and therefore subject to massive vagaries in market
definition terms excuses some of this wasteful activity. The classical
side of the business has less excuse, because the repertoire is more

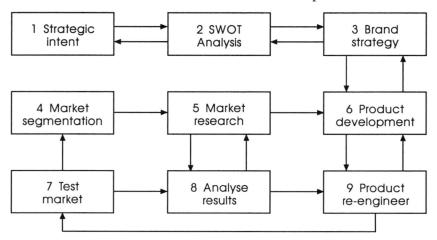

**Figure 2.4** Continuous process of product development

clearly established. Why the industry sustains what is little more than an alchemical process loosely linking the enthusiasms of artists with the buying public, through a distribution chain concerned mainly with margin, stock turn and risk avoidance, is a wonder of the age.

NPD is concerned to push out the frontiers of experience and discover markets that can be exploited profitably. For this reason alone, NPD must be central to strategy. When coupled with a relentless drive to identify the fundamental characteristics of markets, that are likely to be sustained into the future, NPD is an ideal way to ensure that the organization remains responsive to markets, and imaginative in developing them. This is a central platform to relationship marketing covered in detail in Chapter 9.

If Ansoff asks apparently simple questions of market development, Michael Porter (1985) tests our ability to examine strategic development in the wider context of competition. His by now famous *Five Forces* model replicates the conditions under which businesses operate and causes us to evaluate the strength of each force on our competitive position (see Fig. 2.5). The well-informed marketer spends real time and effort in 360 degree scanning of the competitive environment—particularly considering where threats may emerge from and what strategic dilemmas must be resolved. As Hamel and Prahalad (1990) argue, organizations who spend all their time considering their immediate sources of competition are likely to miss the ones that will really cause them strategic worry. Porter (1985) rightly urges us to monitor the external forces on our market-place and avoid complacency in believing that we have our backyard under control.

British Telecom has come to recognize that cable operators, utilizing new infrastructure, advanced image compression technologies and access to programme material, will achieve a disproportionate share of consumer markets before BT can legally enter the fray with its own videos-by-phone service. During the late nineties the distribution of video images will be the most keenly fought-over battleground, encompassing the press media, television, cable operators and telecommunications companies (telecomms), as well as publishing and financial interests. Businesses not yet seen as players in this market have already taken strategic stakes in it, notably the French water and energy utilities, and the US telecomms sector.

The well-informed marketer must consider not only the specific threats to strategy from the existing competition, but also what

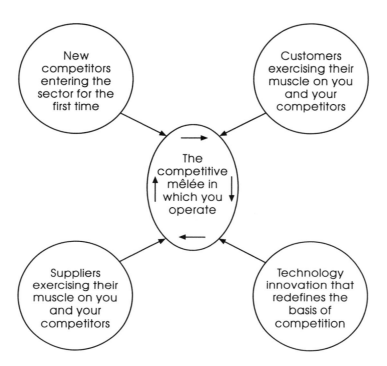

Strategy formulation must be dynamically responsive to this competitive force field in which your business operates—change is always being driven from one direction or another

**Figure 2.5** Five Forces Model .

innovations would permit access to the market by other non-current players. David Llewellyn (1989a, 1989b) has described the concept of asymmetric competition in which it becomes easy for one type of business to enter another sector while the incumbent businesses cannot reciprocate. He cites Marks and Spencer's move into consumer credit not being matched by the UK clearing banks selling shirts.

Generally, the strategy formulation exercise demands close attention to the whole commercial environment, often defined under the headings of political, sociological, economic and technological factors, usually on a global scale that are likely to represent challenge (or even opportunity) to the strategic intent of stakeholders. The well-informed marketer is fully acquainted with these factors and voracious in absorbing evidence of change in the operating environment, whether subtle or dramatic.

When to articulate the *mission* of the organization is a moot point, but as it is meant to be the statement of purpose to the chosen markets and other stakeholders, it seems reasonable to leave its definition until the future potential and core competences have been articulated and agreed. Why then do organizations rush headlong into mission writing, requiring some curiously flexible post-rationalization once the whole task is complete? It may well be that the distinction between mission and vision is not as clear as it might be. *Vision* is a private matter for internal consumption, defining for employees where the organization wants to be, drawing upon its core competences as well as its wildest dreams. The mission is for market consumption and is the aspiration behind the claimed brand values.

Subordinate to the mission we next come to the business objectives—the milestones on the endless road to nirvana—journey's end perhaps? For one Japanese organization (Sony Corporation) journey's end is at least 250 years hence (according to Sony's late chairman, Akio Morita in a television interview in the early eighties). None the less, the progress of the business needs to be modularized to give a sense of near-term focus for endeavour. Even when the goals are in the mid to long-term planning framework, the stages along the way are worth defining: these will include marketing criteria as well as financial.

I shall argue in later chapters that a lack of clear business objectives in the briefing to marketing suppliers is a serious mistake: if you cannot describe the next milestone or two, how can they help you get there? Where businesses need real clarity is in defining the objectives in terms of markets to be served, their detailed segmentation and range penetration. Why this should be arcane data known only to marketers is mildly curious: it forms the bedrock of strategic intent.

Under the heading of strategic options it is generally helpful to have differentiated plans for three distinctive groupings:

- Existing markets
- Competitor-held markets
- New markets.

They are fundamentally different and demand separate consideration. Figure 2.6 shows a model of these three and how marketers can approach them. It becomes obvious at a glance that

|  | **Friends** | **Competitor users** | **Nil users** |
|---|---|---|---|
| Generic strategy | Retention | Establish positive differentiation | Establish primary basis of need |
| Communications focus | Bilateral relationship management | Getting to 'maybe' | Getting to 'maybe' |
| Customer focus philosophy | Consolidate reward loyalty | Optimize 'safe to try' factors | Manage expectations |
| Marketing priority | Relationship management plan | Validating basis of differentiation | Segment needs analysis |

Established customers (Friends) require a fundamentally different marketing philosophy from that employed in persuading Competitor users to change allegiance—the latter already 'own' the primary proposition, they simply buy from the 'wrong' source. Persuading Nil users to buy is a double dilemma—establishing the primary basis of need and your brand pull.

**Figure 2.6** Differential marketing matrix

the most accessible markets are those already held—where the strategy must be retention and organic development—and competitor held markets which at least have the merit of buying your type of products or services, albeit regrettably from a competitor. The last option represents the double assault course of winning the conceptual need as well as the brand argument—not to be lightly enterprised.

Where marketers cannot, I believe, negotiate is in defending (developing even) their home markets. Taking a casual, perhaps disposable view of current customers is still very prevalent. The risk is obvious: if you have lost customers through benign neglect, it is more than likely that someone else has acquired them, perhaps never to yield them up again.

Marketing strategy ought to have at its heart the notion of managing a long-term continuum between the business's core competences (or at least its sources of inspiration) and customer needs. It is, even at its best, a fragile bond and often held only through brand management. If a marketing strategy has nothing else in it, it must have a coherent plan for ensuring that all the customer-impacting resources of the organization are dedicated to the mutually profitable retention of customers. If that can be achieved it is more than likely that organic and incremental development will follow in its wake.

That fundamental coherence applies equally and crucially to the integration of all marketing activities. If a campaign or initiative does not have its roots in this basic strategic intent and is not part of a continuous view of the bond between the business and its current or future markets it should not take place. This puts a massive onus on marketers to integrate the supply-side, so that the powerful creativity unleashed in the range of suppliers to individual campaign targets is cumulative and synergistic to those from other suppliers. Anything less is an unacceptably high risk formula.

In Chapter 3 we take a brief overview of these communications tools and how they might be appraised for their susceptibility to integration within a communications strategy.

# 3
# Sorting the wheat from the chaff

Thus far we have seen the marketer in the role of professional manager, making effective use of resources to improve business performance, understanding the impact of the marketing function on results and striving to achieve high levels of credibility within the management debate. In common with all managers, the marketer operates within a demands, constraints and choices framework. It is the marketer's task to reduce the constraints through developing high levels of competence within the functional team so that more choices can be exercised.

We have also seen the marketer as champion of many aspects of the business strategy, with a direct responsibility for balancing the often irreconcilable aspirations of the principal stakeholders—customers and shareholders. The business strategy is, or at least should be, reliant on the marketer's ability to scan the future horizon for opportunities in the form of sustainable human or commercial needs that can be satisfied by solutions developed from the core competences of the organization. The marketing strategy will, in turn, be a derivative of the overall business strategy, concentrating on specific objective milestones and managing choice using a variety of analytical tools, ranging from Ansoff's Matrix to Porter's Five Forces model.

Subsets of the marketing strategy include clear market segmentation analysis, market research to establish trends of demand and perceptions, brand value development, competitor analysis, pricing policy, product development systems and communications strategy. The latter is the particular focus of *Forensic Marketing*.

In this chapter we shall consider the guiding principles of market communications and their relationship to the marketing process overall. Through summarizing the main tools and techniques we

shall appreciate the scope of the challenge to marketer
sense of this amazing variety of resources. This will h
preparation for the subsequent chapters, which take each
communications technique in turn and argue the case for its
adoption within the communications mix. Each technique's
apologist is an acknowledged leader in the field and has been
mandated to try to take you by storm. For this is the reality facing
marketers: we are the focus for highly sophisticated specialists who
believe, rightly or wrongly, that their specialism is the ideal solution
to our needs. Having a sound understanding of each will allow
marketers to make well-informed assessments of the suitability of
each to the particular situation.

## Context of the communications mix

At the risk of rehearsing old and well-understood principles it is
worth considering both the context for the communications mix
and the nature of communications themselves. The former is our old
friend the marketing mix or the *Four Ps of marketing* (product, place,
price, promotion). Figure 3.1 lays out the basic proposition that
there is a powerful interaction between the attributes of the product
(or service), its price and other value attributes, the market
segment(s) being targeted and the communications used to link
them all. While the model is rational enough and demands a

| 'Customer leading'    Push   → | |
|---|---|
| ←    Pull    'Customer led' | |
| Your product or service array and feature attributes/options<br><br>(PRODUCT) | Market segments you could or do serve and the distribution systems to supply them<br>(PLACE) |
| The financial basis of your offers and explicit terms of business<br>(PRICE) | The communications mix you deploy to reach and stimulate chosen market segments<br>(PROMOTION) |

In using the marketing mix, the sequence will depend on whether a 'pull' or 'push'
approach is being used. The mix should not be used in any single linear sequence, but
dynamically between all four quadrants

**Figure 3.1** Context of the communications mix

thorough understanding by marketers and their suppliers, it is insufficiently analysed from the point of view of its intrinsic dynamics: literally, which comes first?

In Chapter 2 we looked at a very simple model for strategic planning—a basic linear approach in which each stage is a logical cascade from the one before (Fig. 2.1). In reality it is nothing like that, as each stage will have a retrospective effect on the preceding one and groups of stages will have loop-back impact. In practice the strategic planning framework is a complex closed-loop system with many internal loops and exchange mechanisms. The art is to be aware of the whole even when concentrating on one stage: the dependent relationships are the critical factors to manage. It is the same with the marketing mix.

We could start with a product, determine its price to achieve a profit norm, choose a logical distribution system and communicate with the whole chain, from factory to end-user. This simplified linear view is commonly styled product push, since that is what is being done to the distribution chain. In the seventies the acme of product push was the photocopier market wherein box-shifting was the euphemism for pressing the machine on the customer, whether needed or not, so that the long-term revenue stream from paper-supplies and metering charges (the so-called click rate) could be secured. The salesperson's cry was satirized as 'Have I got a deal for you'—deal being the last thing on his or her mind.

Clearly there is a case for product push in certain circumstances, notably when the need for a product or service is so universal that the key task is to ensure adequate distribution, rather than stimulate further demand—the undertaking business comes to mind. We can also sympathize with marketers who are faced with the inevitability of a shipload of product coming over the horizon from some distant factory that is more concerned with production than sales. Here too product push may be the only line to take—moving the product through an established distribution channel and stimulating local demand at point-of-sale—to some extent this is typical of the white and brown goods industries, where distribution channels are well established and retail merchandising is very nearly all, supported by low-level product awareness advertising.

The alternative view of the mix is to start with the segmentation task and identify the needs of specific markets that have prima facie potential, leading to a decision to create solutions for those specific segments or to match existing solutions to them. The aim, overall, is to focus the resources of the business only on those segments with a high propensity to buy. The product pull approach is attractive from this viewpoint—find the need, offer the solution. Now the slogan goes 'Have you got a need for me?'

This approach will include the identification of further needs from existing customers—back to Ansoff again—producing range extensions and upgrade paths, largely dependent on the ability to identify and communicate with those customers and seek a reaction to proactive product propositions. We shall also consider in some depth the ability to clone segments on the basis of understanding the generic attributes of existing buyers—enticingly called psychogeodemographics.

So we have push and pull and combinations of both to manage. But, of course, it is nothing like so clear-cut as all that. The reality is that size of segment, for example, will determine the cost and price of the product and that in turn will have a bearing on the amount of demand that can be stimulated through market communications, which in turn is limited by the amount of resource that the product margin will bear. It is, in sum, a complex web of interdependencies. The questions we need to ask about the marketing mix will include:

- How precisely can I segment my market or potential markets?
- How cost efficient is my means to reach those segments?
- How responsive can I afford to be in meeting the specific needs of segments?
- How will I establish price/volume sensitivity?
- How much influence can I have over demand through market communications?
- How much can I afford to spend on market communications?
- How close to my customers or potential customers can I get?
- What is my competitive environment? How constrained am I on price/performance?
- How well do I understand the buying motivations of the segments I am targeting?
- How much flexibility can I afford to design into my offers?
- Which communications tools will achieve the best response?
- What impact on brand management will this campaign have?

There are, of course, many more questions to answer in deploying the marketing mix, but you will be aware that these questions are closely linked one to another. The overriding consideration is where to start? While recognizing that there are circumstances in which the product and its pricing are largely predetermined for the marketer, I should urge you to consider the merits of concentrating first upon the segmentation and communications quadrants.

This approach ties in well with the concept of being market-led and
market-leading, rather than product-led. Better still, if we accept
Hamel and Prahalad's (1991) advice, is to be needs-led or needs-
developing, so that we avoid the trap of seeking to shoehorn
markets to fit our product. Furthermore, if we place a high priority
on the effectiveness with which we reach and communicate with our
potential sources of need, we may well be able to tap into
opportunities currently masked by product-led orientation. For
example, take the drinks business: a wine producer tends to think of
wine, a brewer of beer, a cola producer of cola and a gin distiller of
gin. Fair enough, but what links them all: liquid consumption,
bottles of glass or plastic, location, some aspects of production
methodology and regulation, consumption environments,
distribution needs and so on? There are profound differences too—
brands, pricing, image—and high degrees of consumer
correlation—beer and crisps, gin and tonic, wine and food, cola and
kids—all of which may indicate other opportunities for profitable
market development. The art and science of this right-side of the
matrix in the marketing mix is to look for commonalties within
segments, rather than product niches. Marketing communications
are likely to be most effective when the whole buying context is
understood rather than the narrower point of purchase.

The relationship between the product and price needs careful
management. The ideal is to develop value-for-money propositions
that are differentiated in complex ways from their competitors.
When the comparison is limited to one or two variables like price
and size the scope for value-for-money communications strategies is
strictly limited. Value-for-money is increasingly being linked to
service quality rather than the intrinsics of the product or service. If
we concentrate on functionality and price we run the risk of losing
the argument for trivial reasons.

Value-for-money is a proposition rooted in perceptions of benefits
received or anticipated: it contains large amounts of irrationality in
its make-up, including self-image, prior experience, prejudice and
perceptions of risk. The marketer is concerned to establish the belief
in the market that the solution offered comprises higher perceived
benefits than perceived costs: the latter includes costs to self-image,
risk of ridicule, uncertainty.

Where the marketing communications tool-set becomes so vital is in
the integration of all the arguments above into a highly targeted,
individual promotion of the value-for-money proposition in terms
of language and style valued by the prospective purchaser. It is this

ability to identify the full range of buyer motivations and to mirror them back in ways that make the individual prospect feel most comfortable that will distinguish the professional marketer.

## Siren voices

We have lightly touched upon the marketing mix and the possible positioning of marketing communications within it. For those who wish to look at this subject in much greater depth two books make indispensable reading: Colin Coulson-Thomas's (1983) *Marketing communications* and Malcolm McDonald's (1984) *Marketing plans*. They explore in great detail the step-by-step routines for using the marketing mix and arriving at appropriate solutions.

That is not our purpose here. We are about to start looking in depth at each of the tools available to the marketer to enhance performance, whether of marketing communications as an output process or as contributor to sophisticated segmentation.

The dilemma that we seek to resolve here is how to decide which beguilingly tempting agency's siren song to listen to and which, like the warnings of classical mythology, to remain deaf to if we are not to hit the rocks. The choice is not quite as stark as that, but there are serious difficulties in knowing when one approach is more suitable than another, and how to integrate several techniques to produce holistic benefit and, dare I say it, value-for-money from increasingly restricted budgets.

The first point to be clear upon is that the professional suppliers to the marketing function have high levels of self-belief and a genuine wish to improve client performance. They have an understandable drive to demonstrate that their solution is the best for the particular circumstance and they are, for the most part, competitively aware. Often the choice between suppliers, especially of creative resources, is down to subjective values—our kind of people, for example, whatever that means.

However, each supplier has an axe to grind and it will be done partisanly—above-the-line rather than below-the-line; telemarketing versus direct mail, television versus print media. So what are the criteria that marketers should apply when evaluating the range of options?

In a fascinating book, *Creative people: how to manage them and maximise their creativity* by Winston Fletcher (1990), the myths and legends are explored: are creative people different from the rest of humanity, do they appreciate commercial reality, can they be managed to deliver results within commercial constraints, are they deliberately stubborn and unyielding when challenged? The answers vary from individual to individual, but some key lessons come through. The most important of these poses the question, 'If you want to be creative why hire an agency?' Another question, 'Who owns the brief?', is absolutely fundamental to the effective evaluation of professional suppliers.

These two awkward questions are central to our proposition that the only way to evaluate the supply-side offerings is to be clear what the objectives are. Note the word *objectives*. The marketer must define the outcomes being sought in hard measurements. To this must be added the pragmatic constraints—time, money, *realpolitik*, and brand integrity management. What the marketer does not prescribe is the creative solution—that is what we pay good money to agencies for.

The disputed territory is often creativity, of course, because we are all human and have strong feelings about such things. This we must avoid at all costs: apart from the need to ensure that the resultant solution is legal, decent, honest and truthful (and brand supportive), we should be wary of our subjectivity.

Where we are sometimes negligent is in electing one type of solution rather than another, perhaps because our experience has confirmed our prejudices. We do need to examine why we send for the direct-marketing specialist rather than the above-the-line specialist, or the PR agency rather than the exhibition company.

I argue that if the brief defines the commercial outcomes, the prior history, the marketing strategy and the commercial constraints, the choice of approach and creativity is almost exclusively the preserve of the suppliers. It is up to them to say how the results will be delivered. Naturally the marketer must judge whether the solution will actually work, using objective judgement. Knowing how to evaluate each solution is what we shall examine at the end of each of the following siren's songs.

Thus we must consider, before listening to those 'sublime lays', what leads to the preparation of a quality brief that will, in turn, yield quality solutions from your creative partners? Here we arrive at the origin of the book's title, *Forensic Marketing*. FORENSIC is a mnemonic designed to ensure that sufficient rigour goes into the briefing.

# Forensic sciences (or art?)

- Focus on facts
- Observation
- Research
- Evaluation
- Negative indicators
- Strategy compliance
- Inertial barriers/factors
- Check and re-check.

Let us take each of these headings in turn and apply them to the preparation of a brief to a professional supplier of marketing communications resource.

## Focus on facts

This is both a broad principle urging an objective stance and a more precise counsel to ensure that you are as well informed as possible through establishing as much hard information as possible about the opportunity being explored. Information comes from the integration or relating of data, and, generally, organizations are data rich—though they may not know it. Sources of factual data include transactional records: what was bought, when, how much, at what price, where, previous purchases, correlative data, credit scores, postcoded address files, decision-making unit records. Other sources of data include press cuttings, surveys, public data (census, electoral roll, etc.), government statistics, industry-produced data, and competitive data. Further internal sources of information or data include the salesforce, service departments, accounts departments, R&D function and operations.

The ability to martial the data assets of the organization is one of the critical competences for marketers, closely followed by the ability to convert data into information. The questions we ought to ask under this heading include:

- What do we actually know about this segment?
- What do we not know?
- What do we need to know?
- Where is the information (or data) we need?
- What interpretation do we put upon it?
- How significant is it?
- How might we validate the assumptions we make?
- Who needs to know what?
- How relevant are the data we have?

- How accurate is our information?
- How do we gather the information we need?
- What format should the data be in for conversion to information?

The list could go on, but the point is made that any new activity is more than likely to be connected with some prior activity and will in turn form the basis of future activity. Every initiative produces a reaction and that will help the organization to get smarter at targeting its resources in the ways most likely to work. If campaign statistics are not gathered in a form that is reusable, ask yourself why not. If you cannot get meaningful market intelligence from your finance function, ask yourself why not.

The focus on facts nostrum is included as the first heading to stress the primacy of objectivity in preparing the brief. There is nothing so dangerous to marketing as the non-validated assumption. Ego-driven enthusiasms for campaigns (including the chief executive appearing in advertisements) are risky to the point of idiocy, when so many hard data are lying around ready to prove the fallacy of the belief. Marketers should be information addicts, endlessly curious about what is known and what are the blind spots.

This does not mean, however, that flair and intuition have no place in defining the opportunity. Far from it. Yet this must be tempered with a search for sufficient information to eliminate the avoidable risk intrinsic to subjectivity. Judgement qualified by fact is worth many times a natural feel for the market. It is not demeaning to the marketer to subordinate judgement to the test of fact.

## Observation

This heading is closely related to the focus on facts. Here we are considering interpretation of information, and the conversion to knowledge. The trouble with data is that they are single dimensional—price paid, product code, postcode, payment method for example—and only when they are combined into two dimensional arrays do they become informative—how many paid cash for product $x$ is quite useful, the more so when compared with how many paid cash for product $y$. Even this level of interpretation falls short of helping the marketer predict behaviour or establish a reasonable prospect view.

What we need are three-dimensional arrays that have time as the continuum. The science of the forensic marketer is to look for underlying trends beneath symptomatic data. The marketer needs to know whether the trends are moving positively or negatively in relation to the planned campaign. More especially we have the need to establish causation behind the symptoms.

Establishing consistent time-series trend analyses for the key performance indicators of the business and the markets is vital to the well-informed marketer. What are the dynamics you need to monitor and what will you do with the resultant information? Regrettably too many data and information are held in isolated pockets throughout the organization, even in people's heads, to be easily co-ordinated into valuable observations. Marketers need to assert strongly for a marketing information system that provides a clear overview of the fundamentals of the business in its markets.

Similarly, the marketer will want to use every new campaign to test out the bases of assumption and to confirm trends. I argue that every campaign should seek to illuminate buyer decision causation and improve the overall knowledge-base of the business. Knowledge is information applied and confirmed.

Decide, in developing the brief, what observations you intend to make—the opportunity is not to be wasted.

## Research

Even after scouring the data assets of the organization and developing quality information systems that help the quality of decisions, there will be conspicuous gaps in knowledge. Running live campaigns to gain that knowledge (or experience analysed) may be too expensive an option. You will need to resort to formal techniques of research.

Feelings are very mixed about research, particularly in general management circles—lies, damned lies and statistics is an old and enduring canard—and yet the alternative is even worse: remaining in an assumptive limbo is not acceptable in the professional marketer, nor in a professional supplier. Research that confirms what you think you know is as valid as research that tells you something new. I say this because it is sometimes forgotten that markets are continuously dynamic: unless you are prepared to check that the goalposts are where you last saw them, you could be in for a rude shock, having missed the match altogether.

The art is to be able to ask the right questions that really yield information rather than mirrored opinion. In Chapter 4 on market research you will see the case put with great clarity.

The marketer is relentless in the search for truth—obsessed with root cause analysis—wanting to know the why as well as the what. Naturally, I expect to be challenged in promoting this analytical orientation: there are plenty who will cry 'analysis paralysis'. A perfectly fair comment and well evidenced if the numerative-based analytical obsession with risk management fostered by some US and European MBA programmes is anything to go by. I do not mean analysis paralysis, simply an orientation that says that sufficient risk should be taken when and only when I have avoided unnecessary risk—the latter being defined as risk that was avoidable if I had asked the right question at the right time, or looked at the information assets of the business to avoid needless repetition of old mistakes.

Without a research orientation it is difficult to see how fundamental shifts in the market can be identified and analysed. You may know that something has changed, but not what or why. That strikes me as flying blind, with only one engine left and fuel getting low.

## Evaluation

The key question here is how will you and your suppliers know whether the campaign has worked or not and why in either case? It is surprising how often performance tracking systems are not in place to monitor change even when the investment in change is very large. This may stem from deeply ingrained beliefs that it is better to do than to know: action is more valuable than thought.

Whether the aversion to post-facto analysis is anything to do with lack of confidence or accountability problems (as discussed in Chapter 1) is open to speculation, but I would ask you to consider the prize to be gained from adding to the learning and knowledge base of the organization through consciously setting out to evaluate what actually happened.

I hold the view that marketers cannot, by definition, make mistakes, only create experience. Their only potential crime is not to learn from that experience. Admittedly that requires the forgiveness culture discussed in Chapter 1 and a spirit of enterprise that values the deliberately and methodical search for knowledge. Given those conditions the rate at which the marketer can climb the learning curve, through structured experience, is likely to be spectacular.

When a direct marketer talks about a 5 per cent response to a mail-shot all well and good. But always ask what happened to the 95 per cent that did not respond. Think why *Reader's Digest* expensively buys a 'No' response in its prize draw campaigns: certainly it would be difficult to justify on the basis of checking that the addressee was still alive or resident at the address held on file. The real value lies in being able to compare the characteristics of those who said 'No' against those that said 'Yes'—the hidden market lies in the difference. If the negative variables can be eliminated, the proportion of 'Yes' responders can be increased.

Similarly, the ability of marketers to obtain post-facto feedback from customers must not be wasted: they know better than you why they bought and whether expectations built were actually delivered. Without this orientation to evaluation of results, seeking to know more after than before, progress will be limited and rather too dependent on luck—something I would rather leave out altogether. In the same way we need to pick up on complaints and poor payment performance: all are symptomatic of problems we need to understand before we seek to fix them. It must not be seen as threatening to the marketer to confront the truth—self-deception is a dangerous bedfellow.

## Negative indicators

I have already touched upon complaints, poor payment performance and the 'No' response solicitation by *Reader's Digest* as a means to establish the gap between the desired state and what happens in reality. When a relationship is weakening behaviours change—for example if you are planning to move your bank account, you may well start by moving part of the account and your salary to the new bank, leaving the direct debits and standing orders to the last moment; your present bank ought to be able to spot these behavioural changes and ask why? How many credit card companies take action when utilization falls off? They are fast enough to move if credit thresholds are breached, but seldom the other way.

Generally, communication declines in quality and value as relationships get weaker. It is, therefore, an imperative for the marketer to know when and why a relationship with a customer or even segment is heading in the wrong direction. It may not, for example, be for any active reason on your part, simply that your competitor has made an offer that cannot be refused—*First Direct* and *Direct Line Insurance* have taken precisely this stance in the UK financial services market—pointing up the difference between what was a satisfactory formula for banking and insurance and what is now possible. Unless this chemical change can be monitored it cannot be remedied.

Negative indicators are arguably the second best condition under which to change the relationship for the better—it is a moment when the customer is ready for change—it is up to you if that change is in your favour or not. The best condition, of course, is when the customer of your competitor is ready to move on.

## Strategy compliance

I have made much play in these introductory chapters on the theme of continuity management and strategic fit for all marketing initiatives. The key learning point is that every sale is the gateway to the next, every initiative is an increment in brand development, every opportunity to understand customer or prospect motivations is a step-jump in corporate knowledge.

This continuum view of the marketing strategy is increasingly important as competitors become more and more effective in niche targeting. The critical competence is the ability to gain the customer, retain the customer and develop the relationship for mutual advantage. With this in mind it becomes axiomatic to state that the purpose of the marketing strategy is to acquire valuable relationships that are sustainable and progressive—that is, adaptive over time one to another, as innovations are normalized.

Underlying the marketing strategy for many businesses is the development of the brand. A strong, magnetic, brand is the key to a long and prosperous business life—especially a brand which is not product dependent, but adaptive and generic to enduring needs and rooted in the core competences of the organization. As I have said in Chapter 2, brand values are earned, not created: it is the perception of the customer and prospect that is all important. Brands are developed through quality of product or service delivery and consistency in their application over many years. Since they are perceptions, however, they are necessarily very vulnerable. Any marketing campaign that is at variance with the underlying values is damaging them. An ill-judged enthusiasm may destroy brand values built up over decades. In the UK this has been particularly characteristic of the banking sector, where tactical expedience has undermined traditional values of financial rectitude. With the luxury of hindsight we can see that it might have been wise if the UK banks, and other financial institutions, had repositioned their brands to take account of the effects of competition and the more aggressive marketing stance that that required. Today, these banks do not enjoy strong brands: the gap has been filled with a virtual spot-market orientation by the market-place.

These themes of continuity and fragility of brand management, within the overall marketing strategy, require the marketer to ensure that every campaign is consistent with the brand positioning and will facilitate the development of relationships: it is increasingly difficult to justify a disposable attitude to customers. 'Win some, lose some' is shoddy marketing philosophy.

## Inertial barriers/factors

In considering the appropriate communications tool-set for a campaign, you and your advisers will need to take into account just how much are you asking the prospect to do. Is it one small step for man or a leap for mankind? I have referred to the 5 per cent response rate to a direct-marketing campaign as indicative of a 95 per cent failure to respond. The question that must be asked again and again is 'How close did we get to unlocking the hidden market?' Of that 95 per cent who did not respond, what proportion nearly bought: 10–25 per cent perhaps? The figure may be much higher if the quality of research and evaluation of past campaigns led to very accurate positioning of the offer: the only stumbling block is customer and prospect inertia.

All of us have experienced post-cheque-signing tristesse—the larger the cheque the greater the tristesse. For significant proportions of the prospect market the inertial barriers to purchase predate the offer: the desirability is outweighed by perceptions of risk. Whenever perceived benefits are less than perceived costs the inertial barriers get higher. Similarly, we tend to bench-mark intended purchases against other uses for the same disposable income, or commercial budget, so nuances of priority conspire to reinforce inertia. The postponable decision comes in the same category: whenever supply is plentiful the inertial factors are at their highest and the marketer has to work hardest to dismantle them, often through the price mechanism.

No one is a fool in their own estimation: if you are targeting competitor-held customers, because your offering is objectively better, beware of saying anything critical of the original purchase. Your task is to demonstrate the positive differential between what was 'the right buy at the time' and 'what is now available from us'. Inertia can stem from an incomplete decision-making unit: hence the insistence of double-glazing salespeople on both spouses being present for the *coup de grâce*.

In designing the brief marketers will need to look for and clearly identify the range of inertial barriers to purchase. One of the imperatives of tracking 'Yes', 'No' or 'Maybe' responses to a campaign is to find the near misses and why. Consider carefully what would happen to the economics of your campaign if you could convert further increments of the hidden market.

## Check and re-check

This piece of advice is, in essence, a reprise of what has gone before. It is a passionate exhortation to make sure that the brief is as complete as it can be, both in terms of objectives and the factors likely to affect the outcomes. The brief needs to be well informed, sensitive to the underlying trends of the market and as well researched as is feasible.

Only on this basis can your professional suppliers optimize their contribution. Be clear what it is that you are asking them to contribute—creativity, solutions, accountability, specific results or advice? Be sure that they are clear what your basis of evaluation of their response is and what they can expect from you in the brief. Too often have I seen agency and client passing each other like ships in the night, not knowing what each other could have done 'if only we had known'. It is, of course, a complete waste of everyone's time if the brief and the expectations it creates are not effectively communicated one to another.

What the well-informed marketer is seeking to do is to find the right solution for the task from among the best tools and techniques available: the first cut at identifying which to use is the writing of the brief.

Now we come to the individual presentations of the major tools in the marketing communications arsenal. Each contributor is championing his or her cause to the exclusion of the others—this is focused advocacy at its best. Read and think about the arguments offered and the claims made. Test them objectively against the FORENSIC checklist.

At the end of each contributor's chapter I pose a number of checklist points and questions. Once you have read each proposition turn to Chapters 13 and 14 in which I shall explore the art of integration of the various tools and techniques and how to prepare a persuasive case for budget. Those readers who are part of the supply-side can compare their arguments to client against this coliseum of gladiators.

# 4

# Market research

## The beginning of wisdom

### Robert M. Worcester and Peter Hutton (MORI)

Since the mid-eighties, while the British economy has grown by only a quarter in real terms, turnover in the market research industry has more than doubled. In this context, though, the term *market research* is a misleading one because much of the research commissioned by private companies and, increasingly, by the public sector has little or nothing to do with researching markets. The industry goes back to the early years of the twentieth century, but really began to grow after widespread publicity surrounding successful attempts to predict the outcome of presidential elections in the USA and national and by-elections in Britain in the thirties. The commercial opportunities for understanding mass consumer markets were soon recognized and led to the setting up of several of the leading market research companies that exist today.

As the usefulness of the techniques for understanding the public's behaviour, opinions, attitudes and motivations were more widely recognized, so they were increasingly employed to assist management in non-marketing areas in both the private and the public sectors, including employee attitude surveys, shareholder studies, corporate image research and the like.

In this chapter we shall be referring to market research to include the social research which draws on the techniques of the market research industry. In this context, (market) research might be defined as

> The systematic and objective collection and evaluation of information about what people know and how they think about, and behave towards, products, services, organizations and ideas.

Most of this activity can normally be divided into one of two categories: it is either *qualitative research* or *quantitative research*. The former refers to methods of collecting information which are open ended and exploratory in nature. The researchers are likely to carry out in-depth interviews or run small discussion groups, normally of around six to eight individuals at a time, in order to understand in some depth how respondents relate to the subject matter under discussion—a new product concept, an advertisement, local council services or a company's reputation. Respondents are encouraged to express their own views, and to react to various stimulus material and (in the case of discussion groups) to other members of the group. The use of certain *projective* techniques, such as asking respondents to describe a product or organization as if it was a person, animal or car, enables researchers to understand how respondents relate to the matters under discussion at an emotional level. An expensive car can signify commercial success, although it can suggest overcharging or exploitation of the consumer in the case of a monopolistic utility supplier. Female figures usually denote caring for the customers; someone who lives in a house at the end of a long drive denotes remoteness from the customer. To be middle aged is usually a good attribute suggesting experience, maturity and reliability.

Many research projects start with a qualitative approach leading to a quantitative survey. As the term implies, the main objective here is to be able to answer the question 'How many people take this or that view or do this or that activity?'

Samples of respondents are normally selected using either *random* or *quota sampling* techniques. These both aim to ensure that the sample interviewed is representative of the population from which it is drawn in so far as it shares the same basic characteristics such as the proportion in each gender, age, and social class category. If the sample shares such characteristics with the parent population, one normally finds that variables which are not controlled also match those of the population. This gives us confidence that we can draw valid conclusions about the population as a whole even though we have interviewed only a fraction of them. The degree to which this is likely to be so depends on the absolute size of the sample (not the proportion of the population sampled) and can be calculated statistically.

As the market research industry has grown, so too have the reasons for using its services. As a generalization it can be said that market research has a contribution to make whenever a manager is planning or making decisions which are likely to affect a sizeable number of people and when information about their behaviour, attitudes or opinions would have a bearing.

## Consumer and business marketing

The most obvious areas for market research are in consumer research. In developing new products, for example, research will consist of far more than just developing a product and getting consumers' reactions to it. Market research is likely to have been involved at every stage. First, it has to be established whether there is a gap in the market and what consumer needs the new product will fulfil: how are these currently being met and what sort of marketing messages or selling propositions are likely to attract the consumer? Leading brands and fast-moving consumer goods (FMCG) in general are likely to have their brand shares tracked using data from the bar-codes collected by the main supermarkets and department stores. This information is extremely valuable but it does not tell you *why* one brand is being bought in preference to another, nor *who* is buying, nor whether they are continuing to buy after their first (trial) purchase. Although research techniques are being developed to do this, currently this kind of information needs further research using *ad hoc* (different sample of people each time) or panel (same sample of respondents each time) tracking surveys.

The equivalent research in business-to-business markets is likely to be conducted less frequently and often one-off surveys are used rather than tracking. The reason for this is that companies often keep closer direct contact with the customer base, many industrial products are sold in vast volume at a time to a relatively small number of customers, and tracking research on any meaningful scale would inevitably be going back to the same respondents.

Another application of market research in consumer markets is in pre-testing the effectiveness of various elements of their marketing programmes. A particularly interesting example of this is pre-testing of advertising.

Advertising pre-tests are usually conducted prior to the time when a campaign is used in the market-place, and are intended to check that the advertising works in the manner which is intended. This allows the client to adjust the advertisement, if necessary, to improve its effectiveness before it is exposed to the public. Because of the amount of money that may subsequently be spent on the media needed to run the ad, even a small improvement in advertising effectiveness can lead to significant improvements in the client's profitability.

A typical test will usually involve measures of the advertisement's ability to gain attention, the extent to which it is associated with the product being advertised, and its ability to communicate the desired messages to the audience.

In addition, some techniques, usually proprietary methods, allow the researcher to measure the overall effect of the advertisement on those who see or hear it.

One example of this approach is the BUY© Test (see Fig. 4.1). BUY© Test in an advertising evaluation technique used in some 35 countries. Over 8000 advertisements have been tested using BUY© Test over the last 15 years. BUY© Test is offered in the UK by MORI. In this technique, respondents are classified into three groups, based on their response to the advertising. *Persuaded* respondents (Gp III) are fully affected by the advertisement, and are more likely to act in the way that the advertiser desires as a result of seeing it. *Involved* respondents (Gp II) respond to the advertisement itself, but do not connect the advertising messages and appeal with the product being advertised; this is considered to be a partial effect. *Recall* respondents (Gp I) can remember the advertisement, but are otherwise unaffected by it.

A method such as this one enables researchers to understand what is contributing to good or poor advertising, and give their clients advice which helps them to make their advertisements better.

Similar techniques can be applied to all other elements of the marketing mix, including products, promotional ideas, and pricing.

This area of research accounts for around 57 per cent of the turnover of the UK market research industry (ESOMAR 1993),

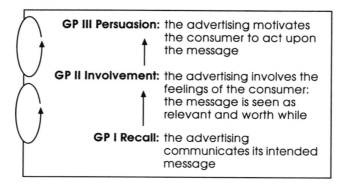

**Figure 4.1** BUY© Test Response Model
*Source:* MORI

though the other sectors are important and growing as their contribution to management decision-making is increasingly being recognized. In sector terms, 33 per cent comes from fast-moving consumer goods, 8 per cent each from media research and customer satisfaction studies, 7 per cent from the financial services sector, 6 per cent each from government and industrial, and 5 per cent each from the pharmaceutical and automotive industries.

## Customer satisfaction surveys

In recent years companies have become increasingly mindful of the cost savings involved in retaining existing customers rather than trying to win them over from the competition. Banks, airlines and the utilities as well as major industrial firms have therefore invested heavily in customer satisfaction surveys.

Customer satisfaction surveys fit in well with the focus on total quality which evolved throughout the eighties and with the requirements of the British Standard BS 5750 (and ISO 9000, a system for certifying that organizational procedures comply with the BS 5750 standard of quality) which an increasing number of companies have been applying for in the nineties.

The value of such surveys is not only in providing hard information on how well customers regard your particular product or service and their reasons for rating them unfavourably, but also in sending a signal to customers that you are actually interested in their views and thereby building up customer loyalty.

## Corporate image

Some organizations, such as banks and petroleum companies, rely on a strong corporate image to support their market position, frequently when the company *is* the brand. During the eighties the building societies recognized the need to build strong corporate images backed up with a sound range of attractive financial products and services in order to compete with the banks when this market was deregulated. A period of high interest rates and strong competition in this sector has seen the demise of the reputation of the banks while the building societies have held firm, capturing market share (see Fig. 4.2).

For other businesses different audiences are priorities for corporate

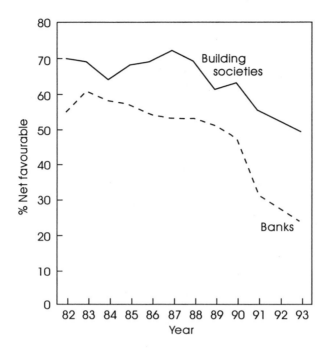

**Figure 4.2** Favourability among the general public for banks and building societies
*Source:* MORI

communications. These might be industrial buyers or institutional investors, stockbroking analysts or Members of Parliament (MPs), business journalists or trade journalists.

Whichever audiences a company decides are important to it, corporate image research has an important role to play in defining the objectives of a corporate communications programme. Research by MORI has, since the late sixties, monitored the reputations of leading companies in a range of sectors among the general public and elite audiences. Two of the key measures incorporated into these studies have been *familiarity*—how well respondents feel that they know a company—and *favourability*—how favourably or unfavourably they regard the company. By allocating values to the question scale points, mean scores can be calculated for each company's familiarity and favourability among each audience. They can then be plotted on a scatter chart. Figure 4.3, for example, plots companies measured among the general public in 1992. Companies plotted further to the right of the figure are better known; those

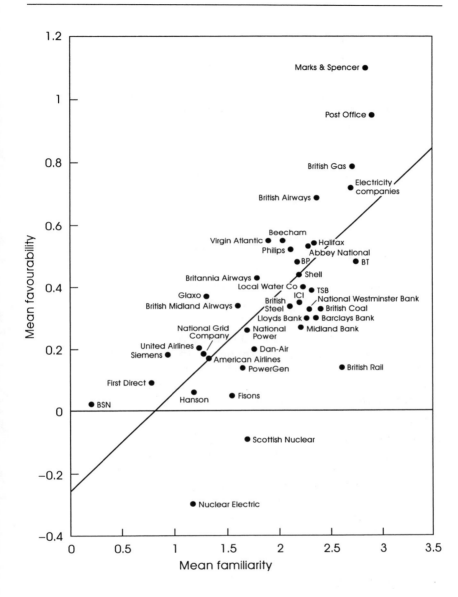

**Figure 4.3** Company familiarity and favourability, general public, autumn 1992
*Source:* MORI

further up the figure are better regarded. It shows how, broadly speaking, the better known a company is the better regarded it is also, although any given level of familiarity can reflect a fairly wide range of favourability ratings dependent upon the company.

In this case Marks and Spencer is in prime position, being both well known and well regarded. Its primary objective is to stay there. British Rail is very well known but relatively poorly regarded and clearly needs to improve its reputation among an audience that feels it knows the company well, warts and all. Glaxo is not so well known but is well regarded by those who think they know it; its main challenge is to increase familiarity and then favourability is likely to follow. Nuclear Electric is little known and those who think they know it regard it unfavourably; it is tarnished by the negative attitudes many people have towards anything nuclear.

Different audiences are impressed by different aspects of a company. It is therefore important to understand what it is that each one is thinking of when making an evaluation of a company. Research by MORI indicates, for example, that City investors will judge a company most by its management, the general public by its product quality, Conservative MPs by its profit and Opposition MPs by its employee relations (see Table 4.1).

Corporate image research is used to diagnose the nature of a company's reputation and determine whether any problems identified are essentially ones which can be addressed by communications alone (e.g. awareness, misunderstandings) or ones which require more radical solutions backed up by communications (e.g. performance).

A strong corporate image takes a long time to build and it is important that this is reflected in the research programme. Thus many companies subscribe to tracking surveys to monitor their corporate images over a period of years. This is done either by using specially designed *ad hoc* surveys for the individual client or by subscribing to syndicated studies, particularly those covering opinion leader audiences.

## Public sector

Research for the public sector has not only expanded tremendously since the mid-eighties, but also reflects the enormous changes that have taken place in the way the sector is managed and how it relates to its customers. The Citizens' Charter, introduced by Prime Minister John Major in 1991, followed a decade in which the roles of national and local government had been radically defined. Since the mid-eighties local councils have increasingly used opinion

**Table 4.1** Criteria for judging companies—spontaneous

Question: What are the most important things to know about a company in order to judge its reputation?

Answers coded from verbatim responses

| | Editors (%) | General public (%) | City investors (%) | Business press (%) | MPs Con (%) | Opp (%) | MEPs (%) |
|---|---|---|---|---|---|---|---|
| Financial performance/ profitability | 42 | 9 | 65 | 80 | 59 | 24 | 30 |
| Quality of management | 28 | 9 | 91 | 71 | 41 | 15 | 30 |
| Treatment of staff/industrial relations | 11 | 11 | 0 | 11 | 6 | 31 | 40 |
| Quality of products/ services | 8 | 47 | 20 | 0 | 23 | 16 | 45 |
| Social/ environmental responsibility | 8 | 5 | 0 | 3 | 9 | 17 | 56 |
| Customer services | 6 | 18 | 0 | 20 | 6 | 8 | 19 |
| Communications/ reputation | — | 0 | 0 | 14 | 12 | 8 | 22 |

*Source:* MORI

surveys to help them to understand how local residents view their services, their communications and the personal contact they have had with them. In this context surveys have a number of benefits which complement the more traditional kinds of information used by councils to guide planning and decision-making. Perhaps the most important is that they ensure that a representative sample of residents are interviewed; thus they include the politically active as well as the inactive, the interested as well as the uninterested in the correct proportions. Great care is also taken in questionnaire design to ensure the questions objectively measure residents' views and behaviour and are therefore politically neutral. This ensures that the findings are acceptable not only to council officers but also to representatives of all political parties.

A single survey can encompass the needs of several key areas of service provision such as housing, transportation, leisure, and waste collection and disposal. Issues which may not warrant the commissioning of a survey in their own right can therefore be incorporated into a survey designed to meet a broad range of needs.

It is now common for councils to commission research into local residents' views, and also to commit themselves to repeating the exercise in future years to monitor their performance and gauge what impact, if any, council policies are having. The London Borough of Richmond, for example commissioned 15 such surveys between 1984 and 1994.

Hutton and White (1993) followed the experience of Colchester Borough Council in commissioning and responding to surveys of its local residents. The research was fairly typical of that being commissioned by local authorities. However, the case study is particularly interesting because it illustrates how normative data collected by the research agency, MORI, over a number of years, have provided management with bench-marks against which the council can determine whether it is achieving its defined purpose. This has been stated as: 'to maintain or improve the quality of life through the provision of protection, regulation and amenities for those who live in, work in, trade in and visit Colchester and the surrounding area'.

One of these normative questions, which measures satisfaction with the way the local council is doing its job, has been asked in over 70 local authorities since the mid-eighties. A survey conducted in Colchester in 1988 found a net satisfaction score (per cent satisfied minus per cent dissatisfied) of +36 per cent. The council set itself the target that it must not fall below the average for local authorities in England and Wales and to move into the upper quartile of such authorities by the continuing improvement of services, thereby leading to an increased level of satisfaction. In practice that meant the net satisfaction level should not fall below +27 per cent and, in future it would be striving for +44 per cent or more.

A follow-up survey in October 1992 showed that, with a new satisfaction score of +65 per cent, it had easily surpassed its goal. This had been achieved by responding to a number of findings in the research which had identified problem areas, not least in respect of traffic control, road maintenance housing, and communications (see Fig. 4.4).

The suggestion that *how* services are delivered can be as important as *what* is delivered was brought home in an analysis of two

Q   How satisfied or dissatisfied are you with . . . ?

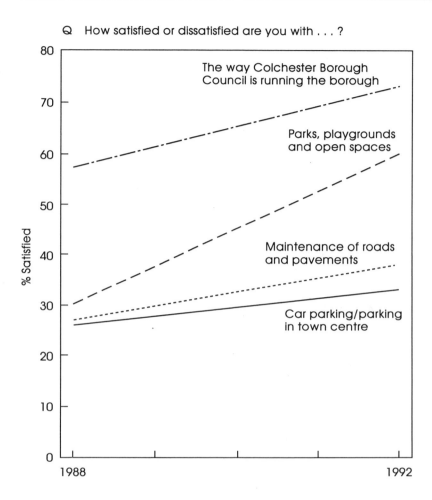

**Figure 4.4** Colchester residents' satisfaction ratings, 1988–92
*Source:* MORI

councils (MORI, 1987 and MORI, 1988) representing similar areas
though in different parts of Britain. It was notable that while the
residents of Richmond upon Thames (near London) rated individual
key services somewhat higher than the residents of Solihull (near
Birmingham), the latter gave a somewhat higher rating to the
overall service provided by their council. One clue as to why this
should have been the case came in the ratings that residents gave to
the contact they had had with council staff. On their last visit to the

council Solihull residents rated the staff they had contact with as markedly more helpful, efficient and easy to get hold of than did the residents of Richmond. There are potential lessons here for retailers wishing to attract people back to their stores.

With the setting up of Next Steps Agencies to implement the Citizens' Charter, a demand has been created for improved understanding and measurement of customer needs and priorities with respect to the provision of services by national government. Research has an important role to play in this process of reorientation. Without the pressure of market forces, feedback from market research surveys provides some kind of measure of customer satisfaction and indications of which aspects of service need to be improved. This is an area of research which still has a long way to go before it reaches the level of sophistication of research conducted for the private sector.

## Utility services

A similar process has been going on in the utility services sector. Although most of these are now in the private sector (telecommunications, gas, electricity, water) they are still largely monopolies in their respective markets. The terms of their regulation, however, mean that they are required to undertake research to understand customers' views about their services and, in particular, their willingness to pay for improved levels of service. For British Telecom and British Gas, which have long been subject to a certain degree of competition, market research is no new experience. For the water and electricity distribution industries such research is a new departure. As in local and national government, the value of such research lies in the new perspective it provides, not only on the individual services provided, but also on the whole business. In these sectors the trend and pressure from the regulatory authorities is towards greater customer orientation in every aspect of the business. Market research is one of the most reliable and indisputable means of collecting information to provide the necessary corporate focus.

Research for the Water Services Association (International Water Supply Association, 1992) in the first few years following privatization is a salutary reminder that public perceptions of service and reality can diverge opening up a major communications gap. Despite one of the heaviest investment programmes ever undertaken by the industry, public perceptions on a range of service measures drifted relentlessly down in the first few years following privatization.

## Employees

Normative data bench-marks are also used in the field of research among employees. MORI has collected information in Britain from a very wide range of companies and other organizations since the late sixties (see Fig. 4.5). Companies commissioning research can find out whether the attitudes of their employees are above or below current norms on measures such as overall job satisfaction, and the company as a place to work, amount and credibility of information, understanding of organizational objectives and commitment to the job.

Because of the extent of the database it is possible to measure trends over time. This can provide interesting and sometimes surprising information such as the fact that, despite the major developments and initiatives in the internal communications field, perceptions of communications has increased by only 2 per cent since the mid-seventies.

Further perspective can be provided by comparisons within public, service and financial sectors so that organizations can measure themselves against others in their field. To be just average is increasingly not enough for some companies which bench-mark

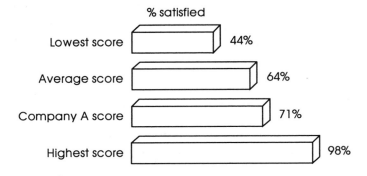

**Figure 4.5** Job satisfaction norm
*Source*: MORI

their performance against top performers in specific areas such as communications and people development.

Another trend in the employee research field is towards the development of an Employee Satisfaction Index, a composite score of satisfaction indicators. This is measured on a regular basis against set targets. Although still relatively rare, this index can be given to managers in relation to their own department as a target built into their assessment in line with other hard targets.

Twinned with the Customer Satisfaction Index, these monitors provide both continuous measures and targets, which have been used by such organizations as the RAC (Royal Automobile Club), TSB (Trustee Savings Bank) and London Underground.

The fact that employee research can be used as a management tool to help bring improvements to an organization is reflected in the impetus behind an employee research programme. Issues at the heart of the business such as quality, customer service, communications, culture and change are all prime movers in these initiatives.

Research in the employee field has, therefore, developed so the reporting structure provides not only data but also perspective and recommendations for a positive way forward to address the issues identified, as well as building on the strengths of the organization.

## Social change

As market research has evolved, so too has our understanding of the power of the techniques involved for helping us to understand social change and spot the marketing opportunities of the future. While the better market research agencies already work alongside their clients to interpret the data correctly, there is a move now to undertake ever more sophisticated research to understand businesses and other organizations within the context of the deep-rooted but evolving values of the societies in which they operate. Socioconsult, for example, is an international, research-based consultancy working in Europe and North America. It advises businesses and policy-makers on the implications of socio-cultural change for organizational development and communications. It employs extensive programmes of qualitative research to understand the various social milieux which make up a given society, then large-scale surveys to measure the core values of that society and how they are changing. The results provide the backdrop for understanding any particular client's business, what this rests on in terms of social, cultural and international patterns, and how this could change in the future (see Fig. 4.6). Part of the purpose of such research is to identify the seeds of social change early on before they become apparent through other means, and to assess their likely implications. Such research provides a valuable link between consultants who are employed to advise on organizational change, though often without research to support their recommendations, and researchers who are specialists in organizational and social change and also understand the nature of the information they collect at a fundamental level.

## Costs of research

Compared with other elements of the communications mix, research is not particularly expensive. Normally the research buyer buys a complete project according to an agreed specification. There are not usually any add-ons apart, perhaps, from some additional computer analysis. Interpretation is usually given for free not as additional consultancy.

Some surveys are set up to cater for the needs of several buyers thereby spreading the overheads. These include general public omnibus surveys on which clients can buy individual question units for a few hundred pounds a time for samples which normally range from 1000 to 2000.

Syndicated surveys also cover specific markets such as financial services or motoring and MORI runs a range of studies among opinion leader audiences, such as MPs, business and trade journalists and the City. These are specifically designed to measure corporate images and the effectiveness of corporate communications and to monitor how these are changing over time.

*Ad hoc* survey costs depend on size and complexity and the audience being researched and can therefore range in price from a few thousand pounds up to several hundred thousand pounds for multi-public multi-country tracking surveys.

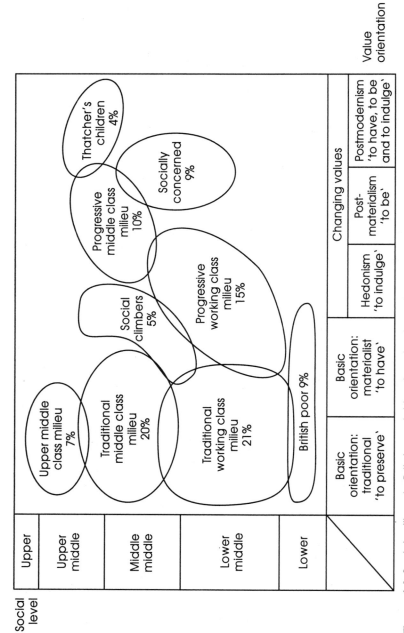

**Figure 4.6** Social milieux in Britain: social level and value orientation 1990
*Source: Socioconsult*

# Checklist

Peter Hutton and Robert Worcester have reviewed a wide range of applications for research techniques in both public and private sector marketing. We now need to consider how their propositions are evaluated. Remember, the key premise for research is to become better informed, so that decisions contain only sufficient risk. Confirmation of what you know, or believe you know, may be as valid as discovering what you do not know.

## Questions to consider

**4.1** What are the current assumptions on which the marketing proposition is based?

**4.2** How valid are those assumptions?

**4.3** How recently have you checked your customers' buying motivations?

**4.4** What do you need to know about buyer perceptions of your business?

**4.5** How well do you think you rate in comparison to your competitors?

**4.6** What factors are you using to make that comparison?

**4.7** How do you know who your competitors are?

**4.8** What are the strengths and weaknesses of your competitors?

**4.9** What do other stakeholders, besides your customers, think of your business?

**4.10** Why does their opinion matter?

**4.11** What are the macro factors influencing your business environment?

**4.12** How will you establish the market potential for an innovation?

**4.13** What innovations are your market(s) looking for?

**4.14** What are the bench-mark standards of performance in your sector?

**4.15** What do you know about interpretation of research data?

**4.16** How credible are the various forms of research in your opinion?

**4.17** How credible are they in the opinion of your general management team?

**4.18** How much should you spend on research as a proportion of revenue?

**4.19** How much do you know about the professional agencies in the research field?

**4.20** How much research on your sector is already published/
available?
**4.21** What priority should you give to customer satisfaction
research?
**4.22** What priority should you give to new product development
research?
**4.23** What priority should you give to a corporate image survey?
**4.24** What priority should be given to a staff attitudes survey?

Those 24 questions will be easy to answer if you are a significant
user of research techniques, whether in-house or out-sourced, but
they will be more challenging if you are not. Knowing where to
start and how to secure acceptance of the value of research in the
management team are critical points.

Give careful thought to what information you already have from
internal systems, such as the transactional data from accounts, and
what information you could get for yourself: postal customer
attitude surveys are relatively easy to distribute with corporate
literature, for example. Be aware that low response rates from a self-
selecting sample means results often have to be treated with
caution. Then, taking Porter's *Five Forces* model (see Chapter 2),
consider what you need to know about each of the forces—
suppliers, customers, substitute products or services, potential
entrants and your current competitors—and on what scale—
national, zonal, global. A particular one to watch is the impact of
technology on your business: the rate of change is so dramatic that
it is easy to miss the innovation that is going to change your world
forever.

Whatever you do, make sure that you are sufficiently well informed
to retain some control over your destiny.

# 5

# Six ways to make advertising more productive

## (Instead of just creative)

### Robin Wight (WCRS)

I spoke to a wise client the other day about the worldwide recession. He said that originally he had seen himself as hanging on to a window ledge with his fingernails. Eventually, he hoped that when things got better he would be able to climb back into the room from which he had fallen. Now he recognizes that when he does the party will be over. The decade of the eighties was the exception not the rule. And that he and his company will have to find a way to be profitable in an era of flat economic growth.

Many agencies have been slower than their clients to recognize these changes. Too many have felt that the good times will come back again. That this is just a nasty blip on the radar screen of economic prosperity.

The fact is, taking a 25-year perspective, one can see that the pressure has been tightening for advertising agencies and their clients for a long time. For a long period, the gap between the amount of advertising a brand *needed* and the amount of advertising a brand *could afford to buy* has been growing bigger and bigger. Consider a few facts. In the USA, in 1965, three-quarters of all commercials were 60 seconds long. They actually called 30 second commercials 'half length commercials'. In 1995, nearly half of all American commercials were 'quarter length' or 15 seconds.

There has been a similar trend in Britain. In the mid-nineties 43 per cent of all commercials are under 30 seconds. But shortening is only one way to pad out an advertising budget shrunk by media inflation. Another is to cut the television ratings, and here we can see the most dramatic impact on major brands.

In 1965 Persil had 9000 television ratings (TVRs); in 1990 it was reduced to 2273. Kellogg's had 7125 TVRs reduced to 2691, Cadbury's Dairy Milk Chocolate had 4111 reduced to 627, Quality Street had 2466 reduced to 1073, Guinness had 4716 reduced to 1415.

Over that period these leading brands had their television ratings reduced by three to four times. It is clear, then, that advertisers are having to ration their ammunition. But what makes all these trends worse is that the evidence suggests that the advertising bullets are not hitting the targets like they used to.

If we look at the market for cars, be it in Australia, Britain, the USA or Germany, we find a rather salutary fact. Even allowing for inflation, it took twice as many dollars to sell a car in Australia in the late eighties than the late seventies. The same is true in the USA. In Britain it took three times as much.

And the story is no more encouraging if we look at beer. Across the world it is taking two to three times as much advertising to sell each barrel of beer as a decade earlier. The evidence, then, points to a reduced productivity for advertisements. Partly this comes from the reduced weight of advertising that has forced brands to operate on inadequate advertising expenditure. (And agencies behaving as though their advertising had far bigger budgets behind it.)

Those big brands of the sixties that I listed above averaged about 5000 TVRs a year. That produced 28 minutes of television advertising a year per consumer for those brands against each of their target consumers. Today, a typical brand is closer to 600 TVRs a year. And that generates just 3.5 minutes of advertising. If 28 minutes of advertising a year could be argued to be a needless extravagance then 3.5 minutes is certainly too little.

New competitors in the battle have added to the problem. In the lager market in Britain, for example, between 1988 and 1994 the number of brands increased by 67 per cent. Each of those new brands is bidding up the price of the existing brands' television air time, and so reducing the amount of expenditure per brand. The net result is a fragmentation of the total advertising market for lager in the mind of the consumer, whose brain—please note—has not expanded in proportion to the number of brands competing for a place in his or her memory.

In this confused fragmented situation, the existing brands have an enormous advantage. Because as the battle rages consumers have tended to stay loyal. In established markets, from lagers to baked beans to soup to detergents, we see that most leading brands in the forties are still the brand leaders today (*International Journal of Advertising*, 1984) (see Table 5.1). Even in newer markets, like lager, the original brand leader in Britain, Carling Black Label, is still brand leader in the mid-nineties. Much as I would like to put this down to brilliant advertising by WCRS, the fact is that brands established when quality differences were more easily perceived are harder to subsequently displace with basically parity products.

**Table 5.1** Leading brands: comparison over 50 years

| Leading UK brands | |
| --- | --- |
| **1933** | **1984 position** |
| Hovis, bread | No. 1 |
| Stork, margarine | No. 1 |
| Kellogg's, cornflakes | No. 1 |
| Cadbury's, chocolate | No. 1 |
| Rowntree, pastilles | No. 1 |
| Schweppes, mixers | No. 1 |
| Brooke Bond, tea | No. 1 |
| Colgate, toothpaste | No. 1 |
| Johnson, floor polish | No. 1 |
| Kodak, film | No. 1 |
| Ever Ready, batteries | No. 1 |
| Gillette, razors | No. 1 |
| Hoover, vacuum cleaners | No. 1 |
| **Leading US brands** | |
| **1933** | **1984 position** |
| Swift Premium, bacon | No. 1 |
| Eastman Kodak, cameras | No. 1 |
| Del Monte, canned fruit | No. 1 |
| Wrigley, chewing gum | No. 1 |
| Nabisco, biscuits | No. 1 |
| Ever Ready, batteries | No. 1 |
| Gold Medal, flour | No. 1 |
| Gillette, razors | No. 1 |
| Coca Cola, soft drinks | No. 1 |
| Campbell's, soup | No. 1 |
| Ivory, soap | No. 1 |
| Lipton, tea | No. 1 |
| Goodyear, tyres | No. 1 |

Source: International Journal of Advertising, 1984

The annals of marketing are littered with new product failures that demonstrate the truth of this. Only 15 per cent of grocery products sold in the USA come from brands introduced since 1970—the rest are over 25 years old. In that period, North America has changed dramatically, as has virtually every advanced society, with new types of products pouring into the market. Many of these products are ones which consumers were not yet used to buying and were far more complex to evaluate such as hi-fi equipment and video cassette recorders (VCRs).

Faced with an explosion of choice, consumers can simplify their decision-making by staying with the brands that they know and concentrate their evaluative skills on the product categories that they do not know so well. As a result, in many markets, the dominant brand leader has got stronger and stronger.

We have now moved to the era of the giant super brands, the new *haves* of the marketing world. The *have-nots* are the new minor or declining brands with their 3.5 minutes of television advertising every 365 days struggling to keep on the supermarket shelves.

With the relative failure of above-the-line (i.e. broadcast or display advertising—all media) advertising to help them, it is not surprising that more and more of them switched their marketing funds into below-the-line. It is something that has been reported particularly in the recession of 1992. It happened again in the recession of the early eighties, but then was abandoned as marketing companies discovered that the new forms of promotion didn't work any better than the old forms of advertising.

Studies amply demonstrate how most below-the-line (i.e. literature, direct marketing, PR, sales promotion and point-of-sale) campaigns at best bring forward sales among existing users. They certainly fail to build the brand values that provide the long-term basis for a premium position in the market-place.

Of course, what is the good of a long-term strategy if the company goes bankrupt in the short term? The challenge for advertising in the mid-nineties is to recognize how the world has changed and create new strategies to help brands in very different situations from the golden years of the fat cat eighties. We need to remember the words of the great Lord Rutherford, who split the atom on a shoestring: 'We have no money so we shall have to think'.

The creative *renaissance* has been replaced by the more demanding creative *reformation*: a new tougher creative framework that needs more imagination, not less. For the business goals will be higher.

But the production budgets will be less. And the media budgets will be less. So we face a difficult task of producing masterpieces with much smaller canvasses to paint on and far fewer colours in our palette.

We have moved to the era, in short, where the creative mind has to be wider than the layout pad. We have moved from the era of advertising *creativity* to the era of advertising *productivity*.

There are no simple formulas that can transform advertising. But I do believe there are some frameworks that can help make advertising's imagination more productive. Six of these are described below.

## Interrogating a product until it confesses to its strengths

All products are not created equal. Research shows that 74 per cent of new products that succeed outperform their rivals in consumer tests, compared to the 24 per cent superior performance among those new products that fail. Yet for how long has the advertising industry believed that they just had to put a new coat of varnish on the product to make it succeed in the market-place?

Now we have to go back to the product and seek to find the strengths that impress consumers and find a way to encapsulate them in advertising. This means going back to the fundamentals of advertising that we had forgotten when we slipped into the big budget entertainment business of the glittering eighties.

Remember 'Washed in live steam' that transformed the fortunes of Schlitz beer in America in the thirties? Product interrogation will not answer every advertising problem, but it will add a layer of extra knowledge that can make advertising more effective. BMW in Britain is probably the classic case history. Since the mid-eighties we have produced over 200 advertisements, most of which have used the grit of product knowledge to create a pearl of persuasion.

It is interesting how companies, like Heinz, have so effectively gone back to telling the basic facts about their products. The fact that their Tomato Ketchup comes out of the bottle more slowly because of its higher quality. The fact that they don't add sugar to their ingredients. In the same way, agencies need to get back to basics instead of relying on what is now an unaffordable creative soufflé to fluff up their clients' sales.

## Advertising archaeology

Many clients have a powerful asset that they are not exploiting: a past advertising property that has been prematurely abandoned. Media costs today mean that advertising properties will increasingly need to be adapted, optimized and modified by agencies.

This goes against the grain of most agencies' beliefs. Danish Bacon, for example, had not used the line 'Good bacon has Danish written all over it' since the early eighties, yet we discovered that 60 per cent of shoppers recalled it. That meant that at today's media prices, there was a £40 million media investment of the past waiting to be reused. And that is why we spent £2 million doing that rather than trying to invent a completely new advertising property from scratch.

We did the same for Sanatogen, in retaining the 'Do you feel alright?' theme rather than abandoning it. Advertisers should now be reviewing their old larder of advertising ideas to see if there is something in it that could be revived. Agencies should be helping them.

## Television posters

One simple way to get more out of your advertising budget is to use shorter length commercials. Most agencies describe this as a *cutdown* which clearly implies that something has been left out.

An alternative way of looking at it is to do what our French colleagues do. Instead of doing it as a commercial that has had something removed from it, they see it as a *poster* that has had something added: sound and motion.

The result is 10 and 20 second commercials that are purpose made for length. In the last six months of 1991 more than three-quarters of the commercials we produced were under 30 seconds in length. It helped clients such as Lunn Poly dominate the airwaves in a way that conventional 30 second commercials would not have allowed. It helped clients like Canon use television which they could not otherwise afford.

Short length commercials can't do all that a 30, 40 or even 60 second commercial can do. But neither are they the second-class advertising citizen too many agencies believe.

## Publi-tising

Publi-tising is a cross between publicity and advertising, and though ugly, it is productive. It means designing your advertising to get media coverage, rather than exploiting it as an afterthought.

Like the way the electricity privatization used the Frank N. Stein character with the expectation that newspaper cartoonists would not be able to resist the temptation to use the idea in their cartoons. The extra visibility this gave the campaign was not paid for by the taxpayer, and helped make the campaign the most cost-effective privatization ever.

Virgin have used publi-tising effectively with their new 'mid-class' by tying in with current events. Heineken and Carling Black Label have made something of a tradition of it. It will be a technique that more advertisers will need to use in the next decade: and that will require a far closer alliance between advertising agencies and PR companies.

## Creating ten-year advertising properties

The ad is dead, long live the campaign: that has to be the maxim for the nineties. The zig-zag of advertising campaigns that gave creatives and clients their chance to leave their mark upon the brand are no longer practical (and they were never desirable).

Creating long-term advertising properties is not easy; it is made even more difficult by the creative pitch that tends to be an advertising zig-zag factory. Our own humbling experience is that great campaigns often have false starts: the first two years of Carling Black Label showed that it was a potentially great campaign but the advertisements were not working. Happily the wise client had the courage to stay with the idea and help develop it.

Agencies will need to learn to be more open, to be more modest and to be more straightforward to create a relationship that has the maturity to support a long-running campaign and not stifle it prematurely at birth.

## Advertising needs to be more than just advertising

Agencies need increasingly to focus on adding value to their clients and not just look for added commission. New opportunities in sponsorship, sponsored programmes and other traditionally non-agency areas create opportunities for agencies.

Like the sponsorship by Sega of the advertising coverage of the European Cup, where 70 different *tops* and *tails* for commercial breaks were created linking Sega into the world of football in an effective way. Conventionally agencies would not have been involved in such a process. But if they are going to serve the needs of their clients they must be involved in them in the future.

People who do not like change will not like the advertising industry of the nineties. Formulas that proved effective in the sixties, seventies and eighties will need to be thoroughly adapted and developed to be of value to clients in the very different and harsher world.

In doing this, there is the possibility that trust, which has been severely eroded in client–agency relationships, can be revived. Without that, and without some of the adaptations—not all of which are new—which I have described has been about, advertising will diminish in importance to more and more clients.

Which would be bad news for more and more agencies. But agency people are nothing if not adaptive. The fittest will survive and the smartest clients will find agencies that have adapted best.

## Checklist

Robin Wight, ever one to break a tired mould, has spoken the unspeakable—the good times are over. Put another way, the ease with which the decision to spend above-the-line used to be taken is no longer possible: the risks accelerate with time, the duration of useful effect from campaigns is reducing and the certainty of beneficial payback can no longer be taken for granted.

Yet the myth is not quite dead. Heavy above-the-line spend remains favourite for fast brand build, despite the decrease in signal-to-noise ratio for each competitor and the consequent increase is cost against effectiveness. Robin Wight makes the salutary point that in spite of the frenzy in competitive up-spend in key, brand-dependent, sectors, no real change in brand positions seem to come through.

The forensic marketer is, at the very least, restless about the continuing low hit rate for new products, especially those brought fast to market with above-the-line fanfare. The truth is that most new products fail. While accepting that there is some inevitability in this, I am convinced that with the application of more science and less (ego-fuelled) art, the forensic marketer can sharply improve the odds of a first time strike for new products—and, in the process, enhancing the probability of costly above-the-line spend producing effective results. How this transition can be attained is very much centred around attitudes to the vaunted claims of above-the-line techniques. The myth of its Utopian power lives on.

We must practise the rigorous disciplines of forensic analysis well in advance of arriving at the range of solutions in the communications tool-set. It may seem a statement of the obvious, but it cannot be avoided none the less, that as the risk factors rise—such as the exponential growth in production costs for TV commercials—so must the preparation effort. After billions of advertising spend over the decades it might be thought that the key learning points had been established to the point that most are taken as axiomatic. Yet it is not so. We reinvent the wheel with prodigious zeal, time and time again.

I am convinced that the root cause lies in the generic resistance of marketers to think long, as well as tactical. Given that every marketer wants to make an impact, and a personal one at that, it is predictable that trying something new is seen as the best way. It is inconvenient, at best, to think incrementally, consolidating gains and seeking improvements at the margin. Admittedly the very best brand-led organizations are spectacularly consistent over time and enjoy the rewards of cumulative communications. They are enviable and Robin Wight's examples merit close study. That said, the majority of marketers I meet have great difficulty in discerning between valuable experience to carry forward and well-identified factors that are positively known to be negative that must be dropped.

It is certainly true that with such powerful media as radio, television and national print, identifying the critical variables in performance is difficult, but not impossible. As Robin Wight argues, a good deal of systematic reflection before new campaigns are even outlined is not just a 'nice to', but the minimum standard of professional behaviour—applying equally to the client as well as the agency. 'What do we know, how do we know it or how can we confirm what we think we know?' are questions heard less frequently than they might be. Is this perhaps a symptom of solutionitis?

Thus, in this the heartland of marketing communications we need a catechism embodying a good deal of rigour in helping us to approach and evaluate each opportunity. The following checklist provides a start-line, upon which readers will almost certainly wish to build their own systematic, and forensically oriented, criteria.

## Questions to consider

**5.1**  What is our prime motivation for above-the-line spend?

**5.2**  What criteria do we apply to judge whether that motivation is justified?

**5.3**  What do we believe the roles of above-the-line communications are?

**5.4**  What is the evidence that these roles are deliverable?

**5.5**  What are the risks that we must appraise prior to initiating above-the-line campaigns?

**5.6**  What are the core strengths of our product/service?

**5.7**  What is the evidence that the market(s) see the same strengths as we do?

**5.8**  What is our motivation for considering above-the-line spend?

**5.9**  How does this approach fit with every other aspect of the communications mix we deploy?

**5.10**  What are the core values that every campaign must contain in order to avoid positional shift (unless wanted)?

**5.11**  What elements must be included in the agency brief before creative work is commenced?

**5.12**  What is the competitive environment for above-the-line in our sector?

**5.13**  Are we adding to the market-place *noise* or achieving a distinctive *voice*?

**5.14**  What are the performance measures for above-the-line campaigns?

**5.15**  How objective are those measures and what systems are in place to deliver them?

**5.16**  What are the alternative communications strategies (or tactics) that could deliver similar performance outputs at the same or higher cost-effectiveness?

**5.17**  How will we determine what *critical mass* is in terms of impact from above-the-line—will we spend enough?

**5.18**  How well are we able to identify variables in the above-the-line campaign so that we can positively learn in order to contribute to our cumulative knowledge?

**5.19**  How well integrated are our other communications with the messages in our intended above-the-line campaign(s)?

**5.20**  What are our objectives in terms of market retention?

**5.21** What are our objectives in terms of new business?

**5.22** Are these objectives compatible one with the other?

**5.23** How rigorous should our agency be in challenging the business case behind the brief and will we listen to and respond to those challenges?

**5.24** How clear are we who owns the business brief and who owns the creativity—does your agency agree?

**5.25** How objective are you really being about your use of above-the-line?

Robin Wight makes a generic call to marketers to consider the maturity of their approach to this, the most dramatic of communications tools. Because of the glamour and the perceived power it is understandable that perceived competitive pressure to use above-the-line, let alone internal pressure, is overwhelming. The forensically oriented marketer will build an objective argument for its use, and will be determined to derive cumulative learning from each campaign as well as tactical advantage. The risk factors are becoming so high that to have any other orientation is, arguably, to take an unacceptable career risk too. Perhaps that is enough to straighten out our thinking.

# 6

# Corporate image

## Credo or convenience?

### Wally Olins (Chairman, Wolff Olins)

## The death and rebirth of the British motor industry

Since the mid-sixties the bulk of the British motor industry, operating under a succession of anonymous corporate names— BMC, BMH, British Leyland and BL—and remorselessly shuffling together an increasingly tired and worn set of brands—Austin, Morris, Triumph, Rover, MG and so on—managed to achieve the unique distinction of becoming simultaneously a national joke and a national disgrace.

During its apparently interminable period of crisis, which derived from a combination of every malaise afflicting British industry of the period, it suffered inevitably from bad marketing. Many of its marketing weaknesses can be attributed to a total lack of comprehension or control of corporate and brand image.

There were constant changes of image policy. A volume car division, called Austin Morris, and a specialist car division called Jaguar Rover-Triumph (JRT for short) lasted a year or so. Austin Rover turned up, only to disappear again. MG badges were stuck on to Metro cars for a bit. A new brand name, Princess, appeared and was then dropped. And so the whole frightful charade went on. Beset by every known corporate disease the corporation did not have time to examine, let alone comprehend, the power of the images with which it was so frenetically playing.

Then gradually everything changed for the better. Jaguar, under a new and vigorous regime, honed its image, became independent and got a quotation on the London Stock Exchange. Eventually, despite the fact that Jaguar was losing money, was wrestling to improve an archaic factory, and that its cars were still plagued with unreliability, Ford paid $2.5 billion for the company. Ford bought Jaguar for its image. Its purchase of Jaguar was a tacit admission that Ford with all its muscle and skills believed that it could not internally generate a brand that could fight on even ground with BMW and Mercedes.

The British Leyland part of the story is also interesting and instructive. BL became Rover. It hived off Land Rover into a different division, and using Honda mechanicals, opted for a niche in quality cars. Gradually its passenger cars started to look like lineal descendants of the old Rover. In this way Rover went back to its roots as the doctor's friend. Cynics might say that the current Rover 400, 600 and 800 series are simply Japanese products with olde Englishe radiator grilles. They are; but it works. Rover dealer showrooms, publicity material and products all reflect the same coherent, corporate image. Rover cars, which look and feel like English cars but with Japanese product quality built in, are now marketed successfully against Volvo, Saab and BMW not just in Britain, but in major international markets as well. In fact Rover has become so successful that it has now been bought by the company whose image it has envied and admired for so long—BMW. These two examples reveal a lot about both corporate and brand image—its management and its mismanagement.

## Brand and corporate image in the struggle for markets

Jaguar and Rover are now as good as their competition. They are reliable and perform well. But nowadays, all cars are reliable and perform well—that is taken for granted. Success comes only when the product is as good as the competition and the image is better. Rover is not taking business away from Volvo because it is a better car, but because it is just as good and offers an alternative image which some people find more seductive. In other words its appeal is both rational and emotional.

## The lesson: choice and the rational/emotional mix

The image issue in marketing is largely based around this

characteristic human mix. When other things, like price, quality and service, are equal or unquantifiable, most of us will buy the product/service which we like better. Emotion is the key.

We all as consumers like to think that we are able to choose between one product/service and another on some kind of rational basis, such as on price, or quality, or service. But price for price, in most areas of the market-place you get what you pay for. In about 80 per cent of the product/services that are marketed today, rational choice is simply not possible. How can you make a rational choice between competing brands of petrol, between the offers of different financial institutions, even between the products of competing chemical companies?

## The vision/core idea

In order to be successful every company has to market products that are as good as the competition in price, quality and service, that encapsulate a clear, simple idea which emotionally differentiates them from competitors, and which some consumers will prefer. Burberry raincoats are sold in the international market-place not only because they keep you dry in wet weather, but also on the basis of a kind of rural upper-class Englishness.

While it is true that the products of most companies are pretty similar, the companies that make them are not. Each company is unique. The vision of the brand or the company has to be rooted either in history and tradition, or in its aspiration. The vision has to ring true and be individual. The vision is what differentiates the company or the brand from its competitors. The vision has to be communicated clearly, consistently and coherently through everything that the brand or company touches.

## Four channels: product, environment, communication, behaviour

There are four channels by which the organization can project a clear idea of what it is and what it stands for. All of these are important, but they vary in significance according to what is being marketed; they are product, environment, communication and behaviour.

## Product

Products and services are what you make or sell. Sometimes the product and how it performs is much the most significant factor in influencing how the brand or company is perceived. It is, for example, the appearance and performance of a Jaguar car which largely influences the way we perceive Jaguar as a brand and a company. The image of Jaguar is product dominated.

## Environment

Environments are where you make or sell your products or services. In some organizations, like retail stores, hotels and leisure centres, the environment is crucial in presenting the image. The core idea of Holiday Inns is most clearly perceived through the environments of the hotels themselves. The way they look and feel is the key to the way in which the Holiday Inns' organization wants its hotel products to be perceived.

## Communication

There are some companies whose brands derive their image from the packaging, advertising and other promotional material which enfolds them and through which they are presented. In these cases advertising and other forms of communication largely convey the core idea. Many consumer goods from Persil to Pepsi fall into this category.

## Behaviour

Finally, there are those organizations whose personality and style emerge not so much through what they look like, what they make or where they live, as through the way in which they behave.

These are, for the most part, service organizations like banks, airlines, police forces, health authorities, and so on. A common characteristic of such organizations is that it is the most junior staff who have the most contact with the outside world and are therefore largely responsible for establishing how the organization as a whole is perceived. The RAC get-you-home service is for example dependent upon its roving mechanics for its image.

# Four definitions: image, identity, corporation, brand

## Image and identity

Although the differences between image and identity are largely semantic they can create some confusion so it is best to get them out of the way. The identity is what the organization projects. All organizations carry out thousands of transactions every day. The people in them buy things, sell things, make things, promote things, write, telephone, meet and otherwise carry out a multitude of activities with customers, suppliers, collaborators, governments and inevitably with their own staff. The totality of the impact of all of these transactions adds up to its identity.

So the corporation projects an identity whether it is aware of it or not and out of this its publics build an image. Even if the corporation makes no attempt to control all its manifestations of identity, its publics will still build up an image, although this image is likely to be both negative and confused. The image then is everything that the audience perceives.

## Corporation and brand

Now let us look at the differences between corporation and brand. A corporation exists in three dimensions. First, it employs people, second, it owns buildings, third, it has relationships with customers, suppliers and collaborators. It makes and sells things, sometimes under its own name and sometimes under other names.

The brand exists only in two dimensions. It exists for the benefit of one audience—the customer. It is the puppet of the marketeer within the corporation who in turn acts as the ventriloquist, manipulates the brand and determines its actions. Sometimes the brand has the same name as the corporation, in which case, when the corporation deals with the customer, it is for practical purposes the brand. More often, though, the corporation operates through a number of brands, which it may or may not endorse with its own name and identity.

# Developing a clear identity structure

In order to sustain a clear, coherent and consistent image, every organization has to develop a logical identity structure. There are three models: monolithic, endorsed, and branded identity. Each has advantages and disadvantages. None of them is intrinsically superior to any of the others. It is possible to find examples of different identity structures among successful competing companies in the same industry.

## Monolithic

This is where the organization uses one name and one visual system throughout. Companies with a monolithic identity have usually grown mainly organically, and they tend to operate in closely related activities. The strength of the monolithic identity is that because everything that the organization does has an identical name, style and character, the organization and its products can be clear, consistent and mutually supportive. In three quite different fields, BP, Porsche, and Tesco exemplify the monolithic identity type.

## Endorsed

This is where the organization endorses companies and brands which it owns with its own name. Sometimes this happens because a company makes acquisitions and finds itself with a number of names, many of which have high value in the market-place. The acquiring company is anxious to preserve the goodwill associated with these acquisitions, but at the same time to associate its own name with theirs. Nestlé, in the consumer goods field, is an example of such a company. It bought Rowntree, whose brands are now also endorsed by Nestlé—the ultimate owner.

Another example is Forte, which endorses hotel brands of various levels of price and quality—Forte Grand, Forte Posthouse, Forte Travelodge, and so on. It does this to show that Forte standards are applied to all of its activities.

## Branded identity

Some companies, especially those in consumer products, separate their identity as corporations from those of the brands and companies they own (e.g. Unilever). So far as the final consumer is concerned, the corporation does not exist. What the customer perceives is the brand. Brands have names, reputations, life cycles, and personalities of their own, and they may even compete with other brands from the same company.

## Issues

Although each of these identity structures is equally legitimate depending on the marketing circumstances faced by the corporation, most organizations, bound by tradition and orthodox practice, tend to follow one or other of these structures almost regardless of evolving circumstances. However, there are some signs that things are beginning to change.

Banks, for instance, have traditionally followed the monolithic route. They still tend to use one name wherever they go. When they merge or take over other banks they usually keep the old name or create a single new name. For example, the merged Banco Central and Banco Hispano Americano in Spain produced Banco Central Hispano. However, with a widening range of financial services—insurance, pensions and mortgages—and the increasing technological opportunity, leading to banking by telephone and similar developments, there is pressure upon banks to develop separate brands which have none of the traditional banking baggage. Hence Midland's First Direct or Union Bank of Finland's Solo are both advanced technology brands deliberately created to be distanced from the image of the traditional banks which devised them.

While a distinct brand like First Direct can be created completely from scratch, with a clear, brand idea of its own, an endorsed identity shares much of the endorsing corporation's image.

The same effect can also be observed the other way round. Some major marketing organizations traditionally dedicated to the branding route, like Unilever and Nestlé, seem to be inching towards endorsing brand ranges because it appears in the long run to be more economical to operate with a corporate endorsement.

## Creating a corporate brand

Although many brands are created, their failure rate is high, and they often sink without trace. New corporate brands are created less frequently, and even then, the success rate is low.

## Q8

The case history of the creation of Q8 is interesting; first, because it is big, second, because it is successful, third, because it is both a corporation and a brand, and fourth, because its development mainly followed an orthodox methodology but ignored it when appropriate.

To join the big league in the international oil business you have to be rich and brave. Kuwait Petroleum is both. In 1984 the company decided to go into the retail petrol business worldwide, which made it the first OPEC (Organization of Petroleum-Exporting Countries) country to move in that direction.

The basis for development was for Kuwait Petroleum's international arm to acquire the greater part of Gulf Oil's European network. By agreement KPI had to get rid of the old Gulf Oil name and symbol. The company opted for an entirely new name and identity, intended for possible eventual worldwide application, linked—and this was another brave decision—to a pricing policy aimed at the same level as the competition.

The images projected by all the major oil companies were studied in detail. As each of them was carefully examined, it became clear that the differences between them were not very great. It seemed clear that there was an opportunity for a major new brand aimed at a younger quite affluent well-educated audience.

Working with Wolff Olins, KPI introduced a new name, Q8 (based on the English pronunciation of Kuwait), and a new symbol, based around the idea of sails and sailing, like traditional Kuwaiti trading vessels (see Fig. 6.1). The name, visual style and overall design of the stations was unlike the competition and clearly aimed at the international market-place of younger, well-educated English-speaking (or reading or writing) audience.

The programme was introduced in the orthodox fashion: first to staff and then to dealers, through seminars, teach-ins and so on. The staff and dealer network, who had become apathetic after years of uncertainty under Gulf Oil, responded enthusiastically to the programme.

The changeover from Gulf Oil to Q8 took place in 1986. Over 3000 petrol stations were involved in six European countries. Just before the change took place the Gulf Oil share in the six countries was a shade under 4 per cent. After the change to Q8 the market share rose to 5.5 per cent. This represents a volume increase of nearly 50 per cent. The market was static so the increase came at competitors' expense. In succeeding years Q8 has sustained its position.

Although there has, of course, been some advertising, the company

**Figure 6.1** The Q8 logo

attributes the success of its programme largely to the impact of the
new corporate image programme.

## Developing a clear corporate or brand image

Q8, Rover, Jaguar, First Direct, Forte and other relatively recent
corporate and brand image successes all have certain characteristics
in common. They are based around a clear idea—a vision—and
they are executed with obsessive thoroughness through the
complete spectrum of activities in which the consumer perceives the
brand.

## Four lessons to learn from these successes

First, be clear about where your product fits in the identity
structure. Is it monolithic like Porsche, branded like First Direct, or
endorsed like Forte Posthouse?

Second, be certain that your product is at least as good as the
competition in terms of its performance, price and quality—the
rational factors.

Third, get the emotional elements—the elements which will enable you to win—right. Be clear about the vision or the core idea. Be certain about what your brand is trying to say and to whom. Try to understand what competitive brands are saying and make sure that your brand says something which is different, attractive and above all credible.

Fourth, pay attention to all aspects of the product and its delivery system. Where appropriate see that environments, communication and behaviour are coherent and cohesive. Most brands fail because they do not deliver. If you manage a friendly and efficient telephone banking brand, be sure that you train your staff so that their behaviour reflects the claim. There is nothing more likely to cause sudden death than a brand that does not deliver.

If you get all of these things right your brand may have a chance, just a chance, of success.

## Working together

The corporate and brand image activity is in the nature of things the result of collective effort between people working in a wide range of disciplines—marketing, advertising, communication, manufacturing, sales, purchasing, finance, organizational behaviour and others.

The rules involved in creating a successful image are strict, but straightforward. They are based, like so many of the rules in business, on the application of common sense to experience and to sound training.

Good luck.

## Checklist

The winner of the British Quality of Management Awards in 1993 was BTR plc (one of the UK's largest industrial conglomerates, including brands like Hawker Siddley and Dunlop), with Marks and Spencer and Glaxo as the runners-up. Besides being voted the best managed company in the UK for sustainable growth in shareholder value, BTR is massively profitable and sufficiently diversified to have a good counter-cyclical capability—enviable and, to all but institutional shareholders, invisible. On the other hand, Marks and

Spencer, besides being highly rated for its management capability, is arguably the most consciously corporately imaged UK business.

Two successful businesses and two profoundly different approaches to image and brand management. That is a key learning point and one well established in Wally Olins's thoughtful observations: we must not think of corporate image purely in terms of street-level visibility. Corporate image is a complex amalgam of factors that include the product performance, the personality of the organization and its voice or communications style. It is open to each organization to decide where its image potential lies, but, as Wally Olins points out, product image differentiation is becoming harder to achieve as more and more products/services become commodity-like. I am particularly keen to emphasize the style or personality attributes of the organization because these have a massive bearing on the way customers feel about doing business with us. When, in Chapter 9, we come to look at relationship marketing, the connection between positive identification with the personality of the brand image and a willingness to remain a loyal customer is absolute.

The challenge of corporate and brand image for general management, not simply the marketing function, is how to develop them in ways which are responsive to changing customer needs and perceptions without having to completely re-engineer them every five years or so and run the risk of losing some of the accumulated values in the process. I have stressed that the business and marketing strategies must, above all, allow for an adaptive approach, sensitive to market, competition, technology, organization and societal factors. The corporate image requires a broad consistency that values the long-view, while allowing dynamic response to changing environments. This is what puts the issue in the realms of general management responsibility.

There are, however, times when an old, and perhaps long-established image is no longer appropriate and requires a complete redesign. That is a moment of truth for the organization and fraught with risk—hence the value of understanding the professional criteria for image management offered by Wally Olins.

## Questions to consider

**6.1**  What are the product attributes of our corporate image?
**6.2**  What are the environmental (point-of-sale) attributes of our corporate image?

**6.3** What are the communications attributes of our corporate image?

**6.4** What are the behavioural or personality attributes of our corporate image?

**6.5** What ought each of these to be to meet our overall business, as well as marketing, strategy objectives?

**6.6** How consistent are we in the application of our corporate image across all functional areas of the organization?

**6.7** How consistent are we in the use of our brand images?

**6.8** How well do we understand the brand attributes as perceived by customers, prospects and other, strategic, stakeholders?

**6.9** What brand attributes are we trying to project?

**6.10** What are our competitors' strengths and weaknesses in corporate image terms?

**6.11** What aspects of buyer motivation, rational or irrational, are we consciously targeting in our marketing mix?

**6.12** How fragile is our corporate image?

**6.13** How appropriate is our corporate image to today's market-place?

**6.14** How appropriate is our corporate image to tomorrow's market-place?

**6.15** How do we know the answers to Questions 6.13 and 6.14?

**6.16** What aspects of our brand attributes do we wish to develop?

**6.17** What are the critical success factors for achieving the brand perceptions we seek?

**6.18** What impact on our key performance indicators does the management of our corporate and brand images have?

**6.19** How will we establish progress in brand development?

**6.20** What is the significance of our corporate image to each stakeholder and why?

**6.21** How well does our corporate image meet the expectations of each stakeholder?

**6.22** What are the core attributes of corporate image that we must manage for all stakeholders?

**6.23** Should we commission a corporate image survey to establish our current position *vis-à-vis* our competitors?

**6.24** Where should the responsibility for brand and corporate image lie within the organization?

**6.25** What could we do to develop each of the four dimensions of image (product, environment, communication and behaviour) to achieve first choice status in our chosen markets and what is the correlation between these dimensions and our core competences (see Chapter 2)?

The corporate general manager, as well as the functional specialist, will be highly sensitive to the prize to be had from achieving a strong magnetic brand and corporate image: they attract business to you and away from the competition or even other applications for disposable income. Corporate image and brands are the tireless ambassadors for your business—they never sleep. They are, however, fragile and prone to premature death if tactically abused: the 'fourth quarter fire fight', chasing any sale at any price, is more fatal than a 'flu epidemic in killing off brands and customers. Arguably it is the responsibility of forensic marketers to ensure that the issues of brand and corporate image are fully understood by, and are responsibly enhanced by, the full gamut of functional areas, whether purchasing, sales, engineering, R&D finance, personnel or production. No other issue is so critically a shared accountability: there can be no opt-out or inconsistency. How much of a battle that statement will create in general management circles I am not sure, but Wally Olins and I are unrepentant in giving it exceptional emphasis in the forensic argument.

# 7

# Public and media relations

## Well-informed publics?

### Jeffrey Lyes (Good Relations, Lowe Bell Communications)

If you run any kind of business you are in public relations. Or rather, you are subject to public relations. You don't need to have a formal public relations policy or programme nor do you even need to make a conscious spending decision. Like it or not, people— customers, staff, shareholders, trading partners—are forming opinions and making decisions on the basis of what they perceive of you: what they perceive of your public relations. So far as they are concerned the perceptions are real. You may agree or disagree—or be completely unaware. But all the time the real experts on the subject, the public, are weighing up who you are and what you stand for. Then they are voting with their pockets (see Fig 7.1).

The decision you have to make is twofold: Do you care? If you care, how much do you care? To those of us in the communications business it is still astonishing to see how little effort some companies put into controlling and directing their public relations. Until, that is, they hit a real problem and then desperately cast around for a quick fix.

It is no coincidence that many of Britain's most successful companies are run by people who take communications seriously and understand the advantages they gain from good public relations. This applies equally in bad times as well as good. A well-known example is that of John Egan, who went into Jaguar and used his public relations skills to great effect to address the product quality issues with staff and customers alike and so turn necessity into a virtue. But when the *Financial Times* runs a story headline 'Good PR gives GM Chief the edge' (as it did when espionage allegations at General Motors' German offshoot flew thick in the air in the summer of 1993) you had better believe public relations has

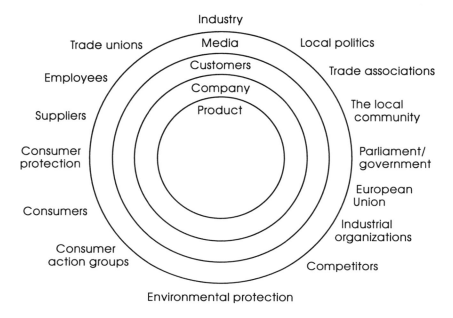

Industry

Trade unions        Media        Local politics

Employees          Customers        Trade associations

Suppliers        Company        The local
                        Product        community

Consumer                                              Parliament/
protection                                            government

                                                       European
                                                       Union
Consumers
                                                      Industrial
Consumer                                              organizations
action groups                          Competitors

Environmental protection

**Figure 7.1** Evaluation of public relations needs to work like a radar—continuously sweeping audiences to monitor reputation and gather intelligence on opportunities or concerns

well and truly arrived as a strategic discipline. Especially as two weeks later the *Financial Times* even front paged complaints by British Gas that the industry's regulator had been 'manipulating the media' rather than minding its own monopoly. Everybody, it seems, can be a PR practitioner.

In the routine running of a business you may feel that you will rarely have the opportunity for such grand gestures or great campaigns. This may be true. But it does not need a big event to sway customers in a buyer's market. A critical press item about a product can begin a process of steady sales erosion magnified by the insidious word of mouth condemnation that follows as sure as night follows day.

A flattering press item, on the other hand, can position you ahead of the game and create a positive and productive climate for sales. It follows, therefore, that a marketing strategy that ignores public relations is at best incomplete and at worst greatly weakened. On a competitive basis major opportunities may be overlooked and on a defensive basis loop-holes can exist through which the opposition can undermine you.

Akio Morita, the late chairman of Sony, reminds us that 'Communication is the most important form of marketing'. Public relations is all about accurate, considered and persuasive communication delivered in a way that is relevant to the recipient.

At Good Relations we formally define public relations as 'the use of third party endorsement to inform and persuade'. The third parties may be either media or relevant experts. The persuasive power of public relations comes from this independent endorsement. In separating public relations from advertising it is not unfair to say that advertising is what you claim about yourself, whereas public relations is what other people accept and understand about you.

The skill in public relations, therefore, is in winning the acceptance of the most influential media or commentators. The audience is convinced because they know you have not bought the endorsement but won it on merit. As a result, an editorial item in a newspaper or on television is reckoned to be several times as valuable—as persuasive—as an equivalent size advertisement. This equation becomes more interesting when one takes into account the high cost of paid space or air time in the first place. Not to mention the signs of *advertising fatigue* that some consumers are already displaying. The video 'zapper' was a wonderful liberator for the advertisingly oppressed.

An independent qualitative researcher, Tim Reid (1993), points out that today's consumers are *marketing literate* to a terrifying extent. His report is entitled (refreshingly or frighteningly, depending on your vested interest) 'They know what you are trying to do'. It shows that when consumer products perform more or less identically, as so many now do, the deciding factors on purchase are the beliefs held about the brand or manufacturer by the purchaser.

Consumers are now looking beyond the packaging and into the corporate values of the brand or company. Anita Roddick's Body Shop is a classic example of the success that can *be built* (if not held) from timely identification with consumer values. But Reid's research also emphasizes that it is not just what you communicate, but *how* you communicate, that the consumer is sensitive to. He suggests that both the content and form of the communication are closely checked out by our enlightened consumer to see how closely they relate to the individual consumer's tastes and values. In this context advertising faces a huge challenge to hit its targets sympathetically and cost effectively. Public relations, on the other hand, can be economically structured to utilize a spread of selected publications with a message tailored in each case to the particular interests of each publication's readers. Public relations thus becomes increasingly useful in fragmented markets where the wastage and weaknesses of advertising become a serious problem. So let us assume there is a prima facie case for public relations and move on to the second part of the question, which was 'If you care, how much do you care?'

Let us put the question another way. How do you want your company and its products to be perceived in the market-place? How important is this to you? Which groups of people matter most to you?

These questions set your objectives and should immediately throw up the parameters within which to consider the role of public relations and the priority to attach to it. Add to your answers a list of opportunities you can see and the possible threats you might face and you are well on the way to quantifying your needs. It is not always easy to be objective and this is one reason why public relations consultants have emerged into the mainstream of business life since the mid-eighties. The perspective of a well-informed independent adviser can be invaluable; the adviser will also bring creative ideas and the benefit of hard-won experience as to what works and what does not.

In addition to your general public relations needs the analysis will probably reveal specific instances where public relations techniques are particularly appropriate. Some of these will now be discussed.

## Exploiting news value as a competitive edge

Your product may have a unique topicality or a performance advantage over the opposition. So you have to make the most of it. Getting in quick via the trade and consumer media will consolidate your lead and create a productive climate for your salesforce or retailers. There is now an enormous range of titles through which to target your audience and a well-organized public relations plan will do this cost effectively.

For example, to mark the fortieth anniversary of the Queen's Coronation, the Royal Mint produced collector versions of the Coronation anniversary crown. Public relations techniques were used to support sales to the public and businesses in addition to an advertising campaign. News releases were tailored to appeal to gift columns in the press and in women's magazines; the product was shown on television and described by radio; a national competition was staged through a Sunday newspaper to award silver

Coronation crowns to babies born on the anniversary. The Coronation crown coins sold exceptionally well and the Royal Mint's sales tracking system proved that many tens of thousands of pounds worth of sales were directly attributable to the public relations campaign.

## Dealing with sensitivities

Being seen to recognize and respond to public concerns rather than burying your head in the sand can turn a potential problem into a demonstration of corporate responsibility.

For example, a US company, specializing in waste recycling, discovered the vagaries of the British town planning system and the power of NIMBY-ism (Not In My Back Yard) when it started building a new plant in Yorkshire. A popular local resident began a Toxic Waste Out campaign and, as press and public support mounted, it was alleged that the local authority had breached planning laws in approving the plant. The case was directed to the High Court and construction work was forced to a standstill. At this point the company sought public relations advice and a four-point plan was devised, to stop the rot in the local press; to get the company's message into the community; to seek endorsement of the scheme from local civic leaders; to propose a constructive way forward for the company and the community.

As facts gradually neutralized media hysteria, newsletters were issued to every household, civic and media open days were held, and a joint monitoring committee was proposed by the local MP. Although the local authority was found by the High Court to be in breach of planning regulations, the judge ruled that the development could proceed.

## Educating the consumer

Public relations techniques can convey a great deal of information. A programme of editorial features and placed articles can, for example, help explain the role of new products and ideas to consumers.

For example, NutraSweet is a branded sweetener and the vital ingredient in the highly successful low-calorie varieties of soft drinks that contain no sugar and virtually no calories. NutraSweet also forms the basis of Canderel, the biggest selling table-top sweetener. A branded ingredient is in itself an unusual marketing strategy and since its launch in 1983 NutraSweet has used public relations on a consistent basis to create and maintain awareness and confidence with trade customers, such as Coca Cola and Pepsi, and millions of their consumers.

In addition to an ongoing programme of consumer and trade media relations, NutraSweet has established links with consumer groups and special interest groups, such as diabetics, and operates a telephone information service for consumers. The core values of the brand lie within a healthy lifestyle and in 1993 NutraSweet decided to reinforce this positioning by sponsoring the London Marathon. New facets were added to the sponsorship by NutraSweet, including the adoption of the Snowdon Award Scheme for disabled people and the production of a London Marathon Book as a photographic record. A media relations team was dedicated to ensuring that the event received the widest possible media coverage.

Although the NutraSweet London Marathon was to some extent a mature promotional device and had enjoyed previous big name sponsors, research by NutraSweet after the event showed that extensive media coverage had sent brand name awareness levels to a record high.

# Adding value to your marketing strategy

Other ways in which public relations can add value to your marketing strategy include the following.

## Projecting leadership

A company or brand that is always in the news is more likely to be perceived as the market leader.

## Changing legislation

Using publicity in conjunction with lobbying can be an effective way of projecting your case—and illustrating the support that you have.

## Promoting corporate values

Embarking on award schemes, giving speeches at conferences or launching community involvement schemes can be effective ways of underpinning corporate philosophy.

## Preparing for the worst

Crisis preparedness is a must, not just for FMCG (fast-moving consumer goods) companies, but all manner of service companies. You will be judged by the public not only on what caused the crisis but also on how you dealt with it. The golden rule is to be as well rehearsed as possible and have your allies well briefed before there is a crisis. This will establish authoritative support for your policies and a helpful response when you need it.

# Opening channels of communication

As can now be seen, a public relations programme is likely to be a mix of the strategic and the highly tactical. But as flexible as it is, you cannot expect to turn public relations on and off like a tap. As we saw at the start of this chapter you are living with public relations, of a sort, all the while. What you do when you formalize it is to open a series of channels of communication. It can take time to get complex messages understood and your audience will expect consideration in return. If you say to the press one day that you are a good source of material they will expect a professional standard of service and ready access to your people thereafter. And they will expect this even when it does not quite suit the marketing plan. So you should enter into the use of public relations with your eyes open.

You might also be tempted by the notion that public relations is a free type of advertising. Certainly the gains in media coverage can be extraordinarily high for the right idea. And, odd as it seems, public relations consultancies frequently undersell their own value. Developing and managing a productive media relations campaign can be very time intensive. This is because different publications like to have exclusive angles relevant to their readership. So the programme becomes a series of tailormade packages targeted to specific journalists, their publications and their readership. The days of a standard press release are all but gone.

Similarly, you must be realistic about the nature of press relations.

The press loves—and needs—its heroes. But it also loves—and needs—to see them occasionally fall. The press loves to be spoonfed an exclusive diet of tasty news morsels, but it also delights in biting the hand that feeds it, particularly when the line between good communication and self-serving publicity is crossed.

This appetite was once prevalent only in the popular tabloids. But it is now visible throughout the press and even in specialist trade press that once slavishly reflected the self-interests of the sector they serve.

Investigative journalism, born out of consumerism, fuelled by political scandals from Watergate onwards and buoyed up by media competition, is now a fact of life. Accountability via the media can come as a shock to the unsuspecting chief executive. Reputations that have taken decades to grow can be threatened overnight, justly or unjustly. In media relations there is no carpet under which to sweep unpleasant truths so it pays to recognize the problems and develop in advance the arguments that justify your actions. Equally, if a company is open to ill-informed comment or mischievous disinformation then anticipation is half the battle. The other half may well be in practising and polishing television interview techniques to ensure you are able to present your case coherently under pressure.

The journalist is an opportunistic sort of animal and as much as it can be a nuisance, this curiosity also provides an ever open door for the topical idea. Your public relations programme, therefore, needs to be linked not only to the marketing programme and the position as seen by your company, but also to the wider events in the market-place and the community as a whole. This will also help ensure that you can readily identify corporate platforms in keeping with the values you wish to be seen sharing with your customers.

## Managing public relations

By now you (hopefully) have a general appreciation of what can be involved in a public relations programme. But two questions probably still remain: How do you manage it? How do you measure it?

On the management front there are basically three options.

First, do it yourself, with the possibility of learning the tricks of the trade the hard way and at some considerable distraction to your other duties.

Second, hire specialists and bring them in-house. They can then get to know the business and the key press very well indeed. But they may tend to become a little sterile on the ideas front with the passage of time. They may also need outside reinforcement for particular issues such as large-scale events or expert assistance on activities like lobbying.

Third, hire consultants and get the benefit of wide experience, an ideas pool, lots of useful contacts and true objectivity. That is, if you pick a good consultancy. The sad facts is that not all consultancies are the same and there are still ex-clients around who have ended up dissatisfied and disillusioned after a consultancy experience.

Interestingly, very few prospective clients seem to ever ask to talk to other clients of a consultancy before they engage it. The formal process of presentations, short-listings and proposals still seems to be viewed as corporately the way to do things, but it clearly has its shortcomings, especially if left as a mechanical procedure. Getting to know a consultancy and its people on an informal basis will probably reveal more useful insights as to their likely fit. Buying some of their time to work with you on a strategy or particular task will give you a much clearer impression with little risk of making a long-term wrong decision.

Whichever option you choose you should always bear in mind that a public relations programme will make demands on management time. It cannot all be left to the public relations team, be they in-house or consultants, as the media will always want to talk to the people who make the decisions. A good public relations team will ensure that the time used of top managers is kept to a minimum and well spent by providing background briefs, hints and tips and doing all the follow-up work for you.

## Measuring public relations

So now your team is in place and you want to measure their effectiveness. First return to start. Judging effectiveness of a public relations programme stems from the precision or otherwise with which its objectives were set, coupled with a clear assessment of the starting situation.

There was a time when the progress of a public relations campaign was measured in column inches. All different forms of coverage in all media were lumped together in a single and completely meaningless statistic. Happily most clients have moved on from the plastic ruler approach, but many still baulk at the additional expense of the more sophisticated research and analysis techniques now available. It is a bit like buying a car without a speedometer.

The true measure of a public relations campaign is not simply how much coverage it got but rather did the coverage have the desired effect? Did it inform and persuade people? If so, how many and how much?

Computerized media analysis techniques can give you bench-marks on 'How many?' and the audience reaction, if you set out to capture it, will answer the 'How much?'

If the campaign was intended to convince people of an argument, then you need to find out if their opinions have changed. If it was designed to encourage them to buy a product, then you will need a mechanism to identify the sales gains involved.

Random sampling can yield useful insights and a consumer information service, for example, can pick up valuable feedback. A small extension to ongoing market research programmes can also capture relevant information. However, the ideal solution is a regular qualitative research exercise which should be provided for in the budget at the outset.

Often one of the most telling side-effects of a public relations programme is the most difficult of all to qualify—a visible increase in confidence of the management team, a feeling that they are a little more in control and recognized as such by their peers.

Well, your overview of public relations is now almost complete. By now some of the fog is hopefully lifting and its relevance to your situation may be more apparent.

The public relations adviser has come a long way since the sixties or seventies. The great corporate take-over battles of the eighties were as much a battle of the headlines as anything else and did much to register the strategic value of public relations with the chairman's office.

At whatever level it is utilized public relations involves a cocktail of ideas, intuition and personal contacts. But be reassured it is susceptible to the disciplines of the marketing world, except perhaps for attaching any sort of unit cost/benefit ratio to it. Then you are dealing in an area that depends on the application of that most mysterious of all management attributes—judgement. And who can put a price on that?

## Checklist

Jeffrey Lyes has made a strong case for public relations as being an all-embracing framework in which the stakeholders of the organization are seen as proper targets for planned and sustained communication—where possible bilaterally. Central to the thesis of Forensic Marketing is the concept that marketers have a strategic plan for the organization that reflects the needs of all stakeholders. The question then arises as to whether their needs should be accepted at face value or be informed by the marketing communications plan—of which PR is likely to be a significant component. By informed I mean checked, understood and balanced one against another so that the resulting plan is sensitive to real needs, perceived or actual, in the entire stakeholder community—rather than an internalized, even paternalized, view of what is best for them.

We need to consider the extent to which PR represents the strategic platform for communications in so far as one definition of it that I use states 'PR is about gaining and holding the high ground of positive image'—clearly a critical condition for any form of relationship management with any of the stakeholders. Another factor that is worth reflecting upon is the role of PR in the earlier stages of the customer development hierarchy:

- *Suspects*  possible interest in your goods and services
- *Prospects*  probable interest in them
- *Customers*  people who have bought once, but with whom there is no dependent relationship
- *Clients*  people who have bought more than once and who regard the supplier as first choice—there is mutual dependency
- *Advocates*  people who provide unqualified endorsement of the goods or services offered—the great unpaid salesforce.

Arguably, in the suspect to customer development phase, PR is the most cost-efficient tool for the development of primary awareness.

Long-standing users of the PR tool-set regard it as central to their brand development strategy, particularly effective in managing the gap between transactional activity—as one wag puts it, 'keeping the bed warm'.

## Questions to consider

**7.1**  How many publics does the organization have?

**7.2**   What do we want each public to know, feel and do?

**7.3**   What do these publics think of us?

**7.4**   What are the strategic messages we want to keep in front of stakeholders?

**7.5**   What are the opportunities and threats (if any) we need to address?

**7.6**   Who are the third party endorsers who can support us?

**7.7**   What third parties would help reinforce our brand position?

**7.8**   How strong is our network of contacts and influencers?

**7.9**   Where are the weaknesses in our network and how can we remedy them?

**7.10**  What public platforms are open to us?

**7.11**  What are the key positive discriminators between us and our competitors?

**7.12**  What are our policies towards the media?

**7.13**  How proactive are we in maintaining continuous relations with the media?

**7.14**  How competent are we in media relations?

**7.15**  How clear are we about what we will say and what we will not?

**7.16**  How much do we know about the techniques of PR?

**7.17**  What performance measures of the business are we seeking to impact through PR?

**7.18**  What performance measures of the business are directly impacted through PR?

**7.19**  What is the relationship between market research and PR?

**7.20**  What are our priority uses for PR in the marketing mix?

**7.21**  What is our ethical stance on external communications?

**7.22**  What value do we put on column inches/centimetres compared to their content?

**7.23**  What do we know about the specific professional areas of interest of individual journalists?

**7.24**  How complete is our knowledge of the media that monitors our sector(s)?

**7.25**  What is our policy on the release of factual data?

**7.26**  What is our policy on the release of opinions?

**7.27**  What are the boundaries of our PR agenda?

**7.28**  How many of our staff are capable of meeting the media effectively?

**7.29**  What is the relationship between PR and shareholder relations?

**7.30**  What do we know about assessing PR consultancies/agencies?

**7.31**  How well qualified are we to write a brief for a PR supplier?

**7.32**  What ought our PR budget be?

**7.33** Where should PR report in our organizational stricture?
**7.34** How should we evaluate the PR programme each year?
**7.35** By when will we have a PR strategy and programme?

Here again, the checklist is not designed to be exhaustive, but in it you will perceive that it is a subject far wider than mere media relations—a graveyard to which it is too often confined. I should argue that PR is one of the most powerful and cost-effective communications resources open to most organizations. It is particularly appropriate in the management of relationships with the so-called minor stakeholder group comprising, *inter alia*, the general public, schools, local authorities, environmental lobbies, local media, prospective employees, suppliers and staff. I make the point because if it were not for PR techniques and resources I doubt whether these particular stakeholders would get serious attention within the marketing plan.

Where organizations sometimes go wrong with PR is in allowing a belief that it is a tactical, even defensive, mechanism only to be deployed in fending off a problem—such as a hostile bid or a serious environmental infraction. First, this would suggest that it is seen only as media relations (which it is not), and second, a tap to be turned on or off at will. Both attitudes are completely wrong. PR is about sustained, quality and, as far as possible, bilateral relations with all the publics we value, or ought to value.

# 8

# Below-the-line literature

## Indulgence or lifeline?

### John Drewry (Drewry Marketing Communications)

The problem for below-the-line literature is that it lacks sex appeal. The very fact that it is often categorized inside organizations as 'print' exemplifies the problem. Indeed, in many cases the funding for below-the-line literature comes from the print budget rather than advertising or promotion budgets.

For lack of sex appeal read lack of funds (when was that ever not true, of anything?). Generally, literature is an area where one side of Parkinson's Law rules supreme: £5 million will be allocated to a television and press campaign with barely an eyebrow raised—major investigation when a sales brochure goes £5000 over budget.

I shall be scoping four categories of literature in this chapter:

- Sales literature
- Information literature
- Internal sales communications
- Corporate literature.

Above-the-line is where all the sex appeal resides. Like films, it is in the public domain, which is where everyone wants to be. If you are on television or in the national press, you are famous, at least for a moment. You expect it to be expensive, which it is. The industry measures up to that expectation in the way it presents itself to you and handles your business. In short, above-the-line is an industry which is based on and functions on big money. No wonder it is sexy. Which is not to decry it in any way. My case is not to bash the advertising industry, but to position literature in your mind as a neglected species, often entirely outside the advertising and promotion strategy, doing a fraction of the job it is capable of, and perhaps even working against you.

Let me give you a simple example of literature working against you. Let us imagine that the product you advertise to end-users is actually supplied, fixed or fitted by trade channels. Let us imagine you spend a zillion pounds a year above-the-line raising awareness of your product and your brand to end-users. Unfortunately, at the trade counter, the contractors cannot understand or cope with your lousy price list, whereas your competitors have sunk some money into making theirs easy to follow and friendly. At this stage (the classic switch-sell, engineered entirely by yourself), not only can all your TV spend go out of the window, but also your competitor mops up the extra market demand you have just created. And what is worse, you are probably not even aware of it. You just spend more money above-the-line.

The reason you are probably not aware of it is because it is extremely difficult to measure even if it occurs to you to measure it. Only sexy things get measured. The effectiveness of your TV campaign, for example, is measured and tested beyond reproach. The response figures are excellent. Conversion, however, is another matter, as you well know.

The price list analogy is easily extended to all below-the-line literature. It is terribly obvious, really. You just have to believe in the significance of it to get worried.

Let me help you. It is a generalization, but basically above-the-line is concerned with awareness, below-the-line with decision. This has little to do with the advertising industry. It is simply the way people behave in an understood cycle of events. At the front end they are susceptible to impression and persuasion. Downstream, at the purchasing decision, is the below-the-line work (or the lack of it).

And here is another poignant fact. You can turn above-the-line on and off like a tap. True, you can leave a lasting impression after the campaign, which is difficult to control or alter. But at least you can withdraw it, or produce a new campaign. Below-the-line, once distributed, is often impossible to retrieve or control. What is more, it can survive an awful long time. It is a physical entity, outside the laws of extinction of tomorrow's air time or yesterday's newspaper.

Literature is there at the decision, the point of sale. It is often the medium through which your company, or its products, are ultimately judged. It is rather like the secret ballot. The opinion polls tell you everything is fine, but what matters is the vote.

I would ask you, then, to view literature as your representative on earth. Earth is where the buying decision is made. But there is no reason why your literature cannot be made in Heaven, alongside your above-the-line work. All it needs is your understanding and your will.

The first rule is to make literature a conscious, integrated and planned part of your overall programme, with a clear view of the job it has to do, and its position in your selling cycle. It is normally the last part of the cycle. Which is why it is often left to the last minute, and left out of the overall planning. And yet, if it is the last part of the cycle, it must be in the most important part. I trust the irony is by now very clear.

In helping you to produce effective literature, some expanded definitions of my four categories will provide a short-cut.

## Sales literature

Literature which sells? Well, yes, but surely everything commercial and non-administrative has to sell, or what is the point of it? There is nothing new about the idea, for instance, that the people who answer the telephone are the most important salespeople you have. Equally, as we shall discover in these categorizations, information literature does a good or bad selling job, depending on how accessible and understandable its information is.

Most organizations I have met have no clear idea of the role of sales literature, or what they mean by sales literature, principally because there is no clarity around the different categories of commercial literature.

If you are to integrate literature into your overall programmes you will need to be clear about the role of each category.

You may discover that you do not need sales literature at all, but that you are sadly neglecting some of the other categories.

My definition of true sales literature is a piece of print which either replaces the salesperson or supports the salesperson. Either way, it is a highly tactile and motivating animal. Its primary purpose is not to look pretty but to shout.

Good sales literature, in my experience, is not handled particularly well by graphic designers. Their role is far stronger in information and corporate literature. Good sales literature is noisily constructed by art directors and copywriters. Just like ads. And only has one basic function. DRY DEM(onstration). In two dimensions, and in silence, successful sales literature has to demonstrate its wares to you.

Now it is interesting how inhibited people get about this. No one would be surprised to see a salesperson hold a product up and say 'You'll be impressed how quickly I can replace the cartridge. Just watch'. Neither would that be surprising in a TV commercial. Or even a press ad. Yet when it comes to literature, clients tend to become very formal and serious. As though it is bad taste or sacrilege to stray outside some invisible decorum (meantime the TV campaign features a man dressed as a jelly, blowing raspberries at a giant rubber duck).

If you really mean sales literature, then get it to talk and manipulate. There is no reason why your copy and graphics should not say 'You'll be impressed how quickly you can replace the cartridge. Look!' That very type of messaging will drive the visual treatment in a dynamic and forceful way.

All too often, however, such an approach will be superseded by a neat square-up in a sea of text and photos, and a little caption which says 'Easily replaceable cartridges'. Now there is nothing wrong with that, *per se*. But it is not sales literature. It is information literature. Information literature is also a powerful selling device. So which do you use, and when?

Basically it is to do with positioning in the selling hierarchy. There's nothing profound about the classic selling hierarchy:

1 Grab attention
2 Make aware
3 Create interest
4 Create enquiry
5 Respond to enquiry
6 Provide information
7 Close the sale.

It could well be that the first four steps are taken care of by above-the-line advertising. In which case you may not need sales literature, because that is also concerned only with steps 1–4. Not all above-the-line advertising, of course, covers all four steps. It may cover 1, 2 or 3 of the first steps. In which case, you may need sales literature to complete some of the first four steps.

Or you may wish to use a combination of above-the-line and below-the-line to create steps 1–4.

In either of the above cases, your sales literature must crucially be themed with your above-the-line campaign. For this to be so, it has to be part of your campaign briefing, not something you can expect the print department to slap together at the last moment.

In summary, therefore, good sales literature concentrates on grabbing attention, creating awareness, creating interest, and creating enquiry. It does not attempt to close the sale. It is not a response device. It is not a detailed information provider.

So whether cartridge replacement is part of it or not depends on whether cartridge replacement is a major benefit or USP (unique selling proposition), rather than an additional piece of, albeit useful, information.

And essentially, real sales literature talks and gesticulates—a demonstration, not a comprehensive thesis.

## Information literature

Most so-called sales literature is actually information literature. But because this is not understood, it rarely performs well as information literature either. The most common hybrid is sales literature without the right uninhibited punch, masquerading as information literature with some ineffective sales subheads cluttering up the information. If you believe you have now understood what sales literature is, then also remember that information literature does an equally powerful selling job, but at a different stage of the sales hierarchy, and therefore with different rules.

Let me sow a seed in your mind. There is no such thing as a 'data sheet'. There is no such thing as 'user instructions'. There is no such thing as 'further information'.

Information is dynamic. It is what people want. Especially at the buying decision. And afterwards, too, when they become loyal and continuing customers.

Information is your most powerful deliverable because, successfully delivered, it results in a sale. Information literature needs to be clear, uncluttered, devoid of gimmicks and smart copy (reserved strictly for sales literature) but—and this is why there is no such thing as a data sheet, etc—its driving purpose must be to inform. Obvious? Maybe, but most information literature does not fulfil this function. Because there is more to it than simply laying out information. There has to be a conscious desire to be helpful. This makes information literature the domain of copywriters. Yet this is not often enough perceived, because copywriters are terminologically associated with sales literature and advertising.

We come back to the same basic irony. Good information literature is often neglected, regarded as an ancillary piece of print unconnected with any promotional drive, and yet is at the very coalface of the decision-making process. Because, going back to our selling hierarchy, information literature is in the second phase— respond to enquiry, provide information, close the sale.

If you doubt this, look at the way a travel brochure works, and the way you relate to it as a reader. Good travel brochures are information-driven, not sales-driven. But they construct their information in layers. Like a gradually focusing telescope, you start by flicking around the world, narrow it down to a country, then a resort, and by the time you are at the buying decision you are studying the 6-point type to see how many yards from the beach the hotel is. You become concerned with the minutiae, the detail. And there is a magic moment when a whole set of facts convinces you.

If that is you at the buying moment, then bear in mind that so it is for most people. Study your experience and work out what it was that made you press the button. Then apply those principles to your own selling situation. What are the facts that really matter? Where is the emphasis? What is useful to know? And avoid trying to sell. Let the pleasure of concise, carefully structured, plain-English information do the selling for you.

And if you want to mark out your information literature from the rest, remember to close the sale. Not with a bland piece of hype, but with a summary of all the reasons to buy. Now there is a data sheet with some bite.

## Internal sales communications

If you think I have already gone on too much about neglected literature, the greatest and most common crime is yet to be exposed, and the lost opportunities.

Let us be clear what we mean by internal sales communications. I mean the literature that (sometimes) gets produced which explains the product, its functions and its benefits to your salespeople, whether they are on the road or on the telephone. It is sometimes called sales support or sales briefing.

Now I have always been fascinated by the nature, and often lack, of communications between marketing and sales. I believe we can identify a genuine phenomenon that has grown up certainly in large organization cultures over a number of years. It is the phenomenon of total about-face. For, incredibly, sales briefing is produced last or not at all, at minimum cost, and as a spin-off to all the other activities.

A proper understanding of sales briefing material will reveal it as the most important of *all* your communications. And I do not particularly mean because it will keep your salespeople better informed, although there are a lot of points to be won there, too. Is it not the land of topsy-turvy to articulate at the end of the marketing and promotional process what all the sales benefits are? Does this mean we did not know what they were during product development, during all the marketing meetings, and briefings to the agencies?

Yes!

Now before you throw your hands up in disbelief and derision, what I mean to say is that articulation comes late in the day. And so, therefore, does a clear understanding of why the product exists, inside and outside your organization. Agency copywriters should not be searching for the benefits and plus points. They should long ago have been identified. Inside your organization.

I am a great believer in scripted demonstrations. For products and services.

It is not just because I believe salespeople work better through training with scripted demos (even if they subsequently improvise, but stay with the structure and the emphasis). It is much more fundamental than that.

I wonder if it has occurred to you that the discipline of having to produce a scripted demonstration provides the embryo for your whole marketing communications programme. I guess it is obvious when you think about it. Working, honing and practising a scripted demo forces out into the open key benefits, personality, emphasis, product knowledge, customer reaction and working messages. You can write your agency briefs from that, let alone your sales briefs. You can produce customer-friendly user guides. You can construct and dissect sales messages and information messages.

I honestly believe that internal communications are the key to external communications. You know the metaphor—the outer person is a reflection of the inner person.

## Corporate literature

Once again, definitions are important. My best definition of corporate literature is literature which promotes the provider, not the provision. If you like, it is a story about the company. Its products (including service and other non-material products) are featured, if at all, only as part of the company's persona, not as products for sale. I think this is safe territory for most people, and the recognized corporate pieces comfortably drop into the definition—annual reports and accounts, company histories, case histories. (People notoriously find case histories difficult to position in their literature hierarchy. I think they are corporate literature. Even though product is mentioned, sometimes in great detail, the thrust of any case history I've ever seen is 'How the company solved the client's problem'.)

There are some fairly simple rules around corporate literature, and you are probably aware of them.

Every established company has a corporate brand image. I am not talking about your logo or your house style. I mean the perception your market-place has of you.

I suggest you research that perception. Among your clients, your prospects and your staff. It may or may not be the image you have of yourself. But you need to know. Because the graveyards are full of failed attempts to change corporate brand image. It is excessively expensive, and usually a waste of time.

The reason research is so necessary is that if you are perceived as a dinosaur, there is little point in producing literature that pretends you are a cheetah. Sure, you may have a bit of a problem, because dinosaur errs on the derogatory. But as a cheetah you simply will not be recognized. Or worse, you may be laughed at. Which would be a pity, because even dinosaurs have their good points.

Dinosaurs, like everyone else, should extol their good points in the way they approach their messaging and imagery, while accepting what they are.

Corporate literature, then, can be said to be about respect, self-respect, reality and truth. Your designers and writers must under-stand that. Use your research agency to help you with the brief. And try to remain objective about it: quite difficult, because corporate literature touches all the sensitive spots inside an organi-zation, and there are great temptations to meddle. Tone of voice and graphic approach should be dictated by your research findings.

## Checklist

John Drewry's championship of the unfashionable but familiar friend, literature, provides cautionary warning against taking any one element of the communications mix for granted. While familiarity and favourability are highly correlated in brand positioning terms, so too are familiarity and contempt when marketing budgets are being prepared. The almost tacit assumption that we shall do a brochure or two, some sales presentation material and the annual report under the loose heading of 'print' is to paper over the fact that this key area of the communications mix is often treated as an also-ran, rather than a fundamental pillar of the marketing communications plan.

Why marketers think so relatively casually about literature is one of life's mysteries. John Drewry argues that it is its lack of glamour and sex appeal. That is almost certainly true. But I believe that the purposes and impact of literature are too little appreciated. While its role is, at one level, simple—to provide structured information that is accessible to the reader independent of any other constraint, such as time or location—its overtones are much more profound. Consider the brand impact. How well does your literature complement and enhance your brand attributes—performance, personality and promotional effectiveness? Great care is generally taken with high spend elements, such as above-the-line campaigns, but literature items, like the poor, are always with us: their durability or shelf-life expose their fundamentals to scrutiny as no other element in the mix. Yet do we think about it in those terms? Arguably not.

Literature is the embodiment of accessibility to an organization. It ought to be exemplary—representative of the highest values you aspire to. As John Drewry trenchantly puts it, below-the-line literature exists to secure decisions: it is the point at which the whole communications proposition comes to the crunch. To buy or not to buy, that is the question.

I sometimes wonder if marketers actually want prospects to say 'Yes'. Is it better to live in an ideal world than to have to face reality? The literature is the last stage in the development of the decision cycle and, thus, it seems remarkable that the ball can so often be dropped at this eleventh hour. Marketers need to think long and hard about the whole relationship continuum if they are to see below-the-line in its proper context.

The four conceptual types of literature offered in the chapter open up the wide realm of possibilities as well as the limitations of each. The single-mindedness that John Drewry advocates for the deployment of each format flies in the face of the widely held view that literature can be multifaceted—serving both the sales and the corporate role simultaneously. Please think again. It is in the focus on the specific objectives for each format that the key to success lies, not some notional omnibus view.

May I urge you to think long and hard about the ways in which literature works: the multilayered process, the cumulative effects, the drill-down to the point of decision. A good start-point is to test your own uses of, and views about, literature you receive: are you led purposefully forward, or taken on a roller-coaster of discovery, including wide detours, or even blocked in your attempt to garner the information that you and you alone want?

Like all good facilitation, literature should blend authoritative fact with creative persuasion, with stimulus for the imagination and gentle nudges towards the right decision. High-level facilitation, practised by great advocates in the judiciary for example, is a seemingly effortless blend of all four approaches; it is, in fact, supremely difficult and, rather as in music, it is risky to improvise if you lack a profound foundation of technique. The same applies to below-the-line literature. Knowing when and how to provide emphasis, and when to back-off is something of an arcane mystery, though susceptible to detailed evaluation and measurement.

John Drewry ends with a clarion call for objectivity—the very heart of the forensic approach. The checklist below may help achieve that.

## Questions to consider

**8.1** What decision(s) do we want at the conclusion of the communications cycle?

**8.2** What is our evaluation of the specific roles of literature in general in our communications mix?

**8.3** What have we learned from our prior use of literature—the positives and the negatives?

**8.4** How well do we brief our below-the-line agency on the macro objectives of the communications strategy?

**8.5** What do we see as the linkages between above and below-the-line campaigns?

**8.6** What proportion of marketing spend should we target at decision-support materials?

**8.7** What distinctions do we make between one sort of literature and another?

**8.8** Do we apply research techniques to the development of literature solutions, such as consulting the salesforce on their need of literature support?

**8.9** Do we put conformity of look in our literature before effectiveness?

**8.10** Why might we do this?

**8.11** What should the consistent elements in all our below-the-line literature be?

**8.12** What are the roles of literature in relation to each other element of the communications mix—such as PR, direct marketing, shareholder liaison, etc?

**8.13** How do we measure the effectiveness of each type of literature?

**8.14** What is the nature of the brief to our agency—measurable outcomes or subjective criteria or something in between?

**8.15** What do recipients actually do with our material—whether internal or external recipients?

**8.16** How important is literature in helping us achieve an integrated, customer-focused organization, through enhancing *internal* communications?

**8.17** What are our strategic objectives in publishing corporate literature?

**8.18** Who are the stakeholders in corporate literature and to what extent should they be consulted in the development of the brief?

**8.19** What are the purposes of the Annual Report?

**8.20** What are the purposes of our price lists and catalogues?

**8.21** What other uses could we put below-the-line literature to?

**8.22** What structured testing can we do to isolate the critical variables in our literature?

**8.23** What pre- and post-facto research ought we to do to optimize the performance of our literature formats?

**8.24** What do we admire in our competitors' literature and why?

**8.25** Where should responsibility for below-the-line material sit in the organization?

If below-the-line literature is as potent in its effect as John Drewry has claimed in the chapter, why does it remain the poor relation within the mix? Its associated subject of direct marketing literature is enjoying a fashionable vogue, due, almost certainly, to the high levels of precision with which it can be deployed and measured. It is the burden of this chapter to say that the same level of precision is available to below-the-line material given sufficient forensic orientation in marketers. The gap is still wide, but it is bridgeable.

# 9

# Relationship marketing

## It takes two to tango

### Stewart Pearson (ADAMAS Partners)

## The business imperative

The concept of direct or (preferably) relationship marketing (RM) is fundamental to business success. It is the aspect of marketing which manages and develops the individual customer relationship. It is crucial to marketing's role as a strategic business function. It has a profound effect on the organization of marketing. It demands new skills for the able direction and management of business.

Relationship marketing operates at a higher level (involving all management functions) and at a deeper level (touching all levels of the business) than the other aspects of the marketing mix. The role of advertising is increasingly limited to creating the backdrop of awareness and image. Advertising agencies—Toffler's (1980) 'image factories'—are dinosaurs ill-equipped for the new interactive world of media diversification, market segmentation and multi-media communication. Sales promotion is the last refuge of the desperate, sacrificing margin to customers and/or the trade for short-term sales. Not only do many promotions not develop long-term share increases (Ehrenburg, 1988), but also in many cases they damage customer perceptions of brand value.

- Only relationship marketing can effect and manage sustained change in customer behaviour.
- Only relationship marketing can target marketing investment for maximum pay-back.
- Only relationship marketing can integrate and focus the corporate effort where it matters—towards the customer.

Today's major business priorities—total quality management (TQM), business process engineering (BPE), customer satisfaction

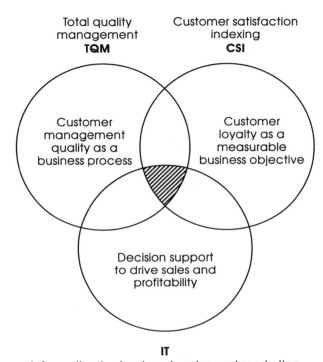

Total quality
management
**TQM**

Customer satisfaction
indexing
**CSI**

Customer
management
quality as a
business process

Customer
loyalty as a
measurable
business objective

Decision support
to drive sales and
profitability

**IT**
Information technology in sales and marketing

**Figure 9.1** TQM, CSI and IT

indices (CSI) and information technology (IT)—are all concerned
with the desire to reorganize the business towards the customer (see
Fig. 9.1). Relationship marketing unlocks the sales potential in these
developments, and redefines marketing as an investment in the
future, not a current expense.

## Direct marketing—and its roots

The term direct marketing (DM) is unhelpful. As coinage the words
are debased by association with junk mail and mail order. We need
new language for this most dynamic business concept.

Its roots do lie in mail order as a channel of distribution, and direct
mail as a communication medium to support this channel. The
pioneers of DM in the fifties were *Reader's Digest* and the mail order
catalogues. Then in the seventies financial and business marketers

(from American Express to IBM) recognized its potential. In the nineties the degree of commitment of any business to the concept is a measure of its forward thinking—and of its chances of survival.

Every business needs DM—because every business needs customers.

## Relationship marketing—and the new language

DM is the fastest growing force in marketing. You cannot measure DM, because it is a concept, and not just a medium or a channel. But you can measure the explosive growth in direct mail, in direct response advertising, in customer databases, in the use of the telephone in marketing, and above all in the new focus on customer retention and loyalty. And the movement is not unique to the USA, but is now gathering momentum throughout Europe (EDMA/NTC Research 1993) (EDMA is the acronym of the European Direct Marketing Association). Expenditure on DM is estimated at 27 billion ECUs (growth rate 8 per cent per year) against media advertising at 37.4 billion ECUs (set to decline).

One simple idea drives all these developments. The role of marketing in business is to create and deliver to customer needs. Business success rests on customer relationships. Marketing's objective is to generate business value by developing the value of customer relationships.

As Levitt (1983) puts it succinctly: 'the purpose of business is to make and keep a customer'.

## The value of the customer—and what you must know

The value of the customer is the contribution to profit which flows from the revenue streams generated from customer relationships. The concept is best illustrated by example, and the calculation is guaranteed to challenge your imagination. Do it now—even if only on the back of an envelope.

Think of yourself first, as a customer perhaps of your favourite restaurant. Think of the value of your custom—how much you spend each month, each year, in the last five years. Then think about family and friends you might have recommended to it. Then think about what might happen if you stopped visiting, if you had an unpleasant experience, if you told others about it. Just how much are you worth as a customer over five years? (Tom Peters (1987) uses this example to telling effect.)

This is your value as a customer.

How much might you be worth if you went more regularly? Do you receive the service you deserve? Do you feel special? Do they talk to you about changes? If they advertise do they talk to you first? Do they create special events or experiences for you?

How much will it cost them if they upset you?

Keep thinking about yourself as a customer—but now of your bank, your insurance company, your supermarket, your fashion store—the manufacturers of all the products you buy from day-to-day, from week-to-week. Think of the major suppliers to your business. How much were you worth to them over the last five years—and how much might you be worth over the next five?

Then think about the value of your customers.

# The value of relationships—and the implications

All business revenue flows from customer transactions. The quality and reliability of this revenue depends fundamentally on the quality of customer relationships.

Value is sometimes attributed to brands, with some companies putting the value of their brands on their balance sheet. But the accounting value of a brand is only the discounted cash flow from anticipated future purchases of the brand by today's customers. What counts is customer behaviour, and it is changes in customer behaviour (towards new brands and own label) which threaten any brand, from soap powder to computers.

The value of a brand can only be attributed to the value placed by the customer—and the effect on future purchase choice.

Value lies in customers, not brands. And marketers who calculate the value of the customer for one brand or product ignore the potential value of all household or business transactions for all their brands, products and services.

Value is sometime maintained by personal relationships. Salesforces and retailers deliver the products and services, and are the immediate interface with the customer. But it is customer information, and signals relayed from the personal relationship which matter in retaining and developing the customer. These signals become the basis of the dynamic customer databases which increasingly drive marketing actions.

Value lies in the feedback from the relationship, not simply the personal contact. So marketers who rely on salesforces, agents, dealers and re-sellers are vulnerable if they do not receive the flow of information and signals which will enable them to own the customer.

The value of the customer has profound implications for marketing strategy. The message is clear, that retention of customers and development of relationships is the business priority—not only because it is essential to ensure business survival, but also because it pays. Indeed nothing pays quite like it.

The evidence is everywhere. Price Waterhouse (1993) has calculated that a 2 per cent increase in customer retention is equivalent to a 10 per cent reduction in costs—and is a much better way of surviving recession. In the US, TARP (1988) (Technical Assistance Research Programmes) has researched customer satisfaction and report that addressing a customer complaint raises re-purchase rates even where the complaint is not fully resolved. Bain (quoted in Reichfeld, 1993) reports re-purchase rates rising uniformly with the length of a relationship—and concomitantly that bank branch profitability rises with the length of tenure of the manager.

We need a new perspective—that of the customer.

Any business that studies its sales from this new perspective finds that it costs from four to twelve times more to sell to a new customer as to an existing one. A shift in focus to customers can transform marketing effectiveness at a stroke.

## Relationship marketing—the business model

The business model for relationship marketing can be best represented as a Spiral of Prosperity, in which the organization creates and generates value from customer relationships (see Fig. 9.2).

### Customer prospecting—opening the relationship

Customer prospecting is the highly targeted recruitment of

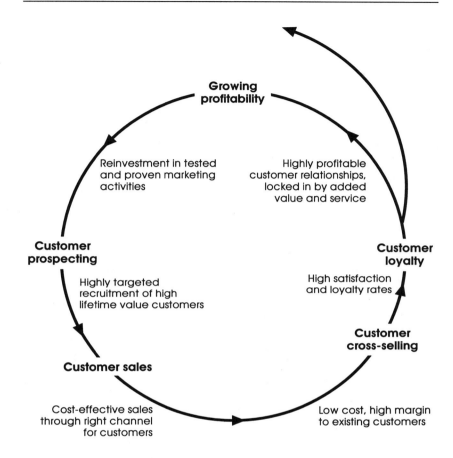

**Figure 9.2** Spiral of prosperity

customers—not just any customers but market segments with high lifetime value potential. Prospecting replaces the mass advertising approach to new business with strategic identification of the most profitable parts of the market, the competitive customers who are worth attacking cost effectively, and the segments with real long-term futures. Prospecting generates a database of potential recruits for today and tomorrow.

Increasingly marketers are using direct response advertising and direct promotions to prospect and to build databases. A famous example is the 'World's Biggest Offer' by British Airways. By creating a motivating proposition prospecting has been used in markets as diverse as pet foods and computers. The critical success factor is a motivating proposition to 'engage' the prospective customer.

## Customer sales

Customer sales matches message, offer and channel to customer. The database system of potential recruits drives the selection of the right message at the right time, delivered with the right offer through the right channel, to maximize cost-effective sales. Communication is managed by the design of a cost-effective contact strategy which selects customers for appropriate cost-effective contact which is timed, targeted and triggered by the system. The process involves both 'pull' (targeted messages to customers) and 'push' (tailored support packages to the field, to the trade, and to retailers). All channels of distribution can be supported, with direct distribution (home shopping) offering the exciting potential in any market for incremental sales through a new channel.

Increasingly marketers are identifying their end-customer directly, however the sale is ultimately made. A famous example of a business founded on a direct channel is Dell Computer. Markets as diverse as entertainment and financial services are developing new direct channels and new revenue streams, complementary to their existing distribution networks.

## Customer cross-selling

Customer cross-selling begins the process of developing the customer relationship by determining in partnership with the customer—and driven by the customer—the future products and services which the customer needs and might buy. Cross-selling is driven by learning about the customer, identifying needs, and choosing the right timing to address these needs. Not only is selling more to existing customers (as noted above) highly cost effective, but also it is essential to move from a single transaction or product relationship.

Increasingly marketers are redirecting their creativity and spend, away from general advertising, and to their customers. A famous example of commitment to customers has always been American Express. By moving from isolated mailings to a series of messages that identify and meet the needs of selected customers, any company can create more profitable relationships and more satisfied customers.

## Customer loyalty

Customer loyalty is whatever locks-in the customer to the business. Loyalty is another term in danger of debasement to nothing more than a promotional scheme. Loyalty has two levels. At the first level the rewards are *functional*—the financial rewards and additional product benefits the customer receives for repeated and frequent buying. But there must also be a second *emotional* level to loyalty, arising from recognition of the customer and enhanced levels of service and customer care. Loyalty will demand that the business treats the customer as an individual, with all that this entails, and that the customer recognizes the human touch.

Increasingly marketers are differentiating their proposition and adding value to their service to regular users, to enhance loyalty. The successful loyalty programmes are more than elaborate promotions or discounting. Customer tracking studies, just like advertising tracking, can be used to evaluate the return on investment from loyalty, as well as the incremental sales.

# Relationship marketing—the art

The concept of a brand has three dimensions—features, benefits, and added values. The relationship with the customer now becomes an essential fourth dimension. The nature of and motivation for the relationship defines and develops the brand position and role in the customer's life.

There is a magic moment when customers make direct contact with a business, and learn that the business is organized and willing to treat them as individuals. The creative process in relationship marketing then becomes a development of general or brand advertising, but now the customer is directly involved or (better language) engaged, and no longer the passive onlooker at broadcast and space media. The brand personality is reaffirmed ever more strongly when it reacts directly with the customer.

The engagement creates the opportunity to sense customer needs and to select appropriate messages. Once the customer responds, future communications become solicited, and ideally welcome. Any response—no matter how modest—becomes the start of a relationship. Companies who put the customer first can enjoy a genuine advantage over more passive competitors.

## Relationship marketing—and the integration of other activities

In the business model relationship marketing may exploit the high awareness and positive image created by general advertising and public relations. But even this is only a model appropriate to mass brands. It is increasingly inappropriate in the new media environment, and less and less economic for a broader range of businesses.

Increasingly the role of advertising is to recruit: it is a matter of observation that the majority of advertising now carries a response device, and direct response television is a wave of the future. Targeted customer communications carry the responsibility not only of selling but also of achieving advertising objectives— generating awareness, fostering a positive image and creating preference.

And the new proliferation of media channels—only just underway in Europe—will change the very nature of the media. A visit to the USA is no longer needed to observe how 'junk' television is an increasingly inappropriate environment for brand-building, and how media choice makes buying your target audience impossibly expensive and complex.

In the business model the role of promotions is also to recruit. This means that promotions must become targeted to segments with profit potential. They must discriminate between user and non-users. They must be designed as the first step in a customer relationship and not as a one-off transaction. They must be planned to generate return-on-investment. Promotions are not a separate activity but an element of the relationship marketing process.

## Relationship marketing—and organizational resources

Business faces a bewildering choice today in selection of its marketing agents and suppliers. Advertising agencies of all structures and philosophies vie with direct marketing agencies, sales promotion agencies, public relations consultants, management consultants as well as a new range of service bureaux specializing in data processing, mail and telephone. There must be consolidation, and the shape of the consolidation will reflect the imperatives of business.

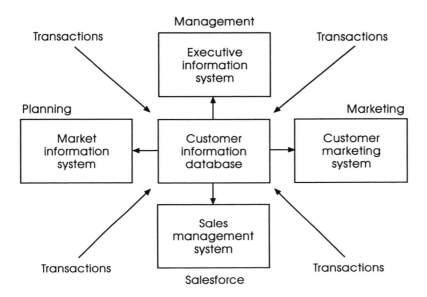

**Figure 9.3** Customer support system

The first development will be that business will internalize more and more of the process functions of relationship marketing. The organizational structure will develop to accommodate two major functions—the customer support system (CSS) and the customer contact centre (CCC).

The CSS is the evolution of the customer database concept towards a system in which all functions in the organization access and manage customer information (see Fig. 9.3). Increasingly the customer too will access the CSS (which is just what is happening, for example, in the rapid trend towards more cost-effective remote banking).

The CCC is the integration of the customer response concept with customer communications so that it becomes practicable and manageable to respond to customer needs on an individual basis. The CCC will encompass telephone and mail response management. In the future it will offer on-line access through electronic media. It will be cost-justified on the basis of increased customer retention (by satisfying the problems of customers) and of increased customer cross-selling (by providing customers with direct access). It will become a source of competitive advantage, winning and retaining customers by providing easier access and superior service.

## Relationship marketing—and service sector structure

The advertising industry sector in the USA and Europe is struggling to respond to the changes in client needs which are eroding its value to business. Since the early seventies it has attempted to retain its hold on client relationships by diversifying, and in particular by acquiring other marketing services functions.

That strategy has failed. In particular the attempt by advertising and promotion agencies to hijack direct marketing, with its totally different skills and philosophies, has set back development by years. There was no client benefit in the one-stop shop.

In the future business will work with two forms of external agencies. First, the advertising agency will survive, alongside an autonomous but dependent media buying service. The role of the agency will be much curtailed to a source of creative ideas, and its assignments will be mass market brands.

The second form of agency will be the relationship marketing agency. The services of this agency will be direct response advertising, sales support, customer communications and customer loyalty. The value added will be deep and objective customer understanding, derived from a balanced tool-kit of qualitative and quantitative skills. Communication programmes will be designed through a new data-driven planning system.

This agency and its clients will both have on-line access to customer information, and the tools to use this information to guide decision-making and to manage marketing programmes. There will be no separate account, creative, media and production departments: clients will have dedicated business teams with an integrated set of planning, communication, sales and project management skills (see Fig. 9.4).

This agency will be specifically skilled in the development of interactive communications between business and its customers using the new interactive media, through satellite, cable and telephone lines into the customer's business and home.

## Relationship marketing—and business organization

Relationship marketing will have significant effects on marketing

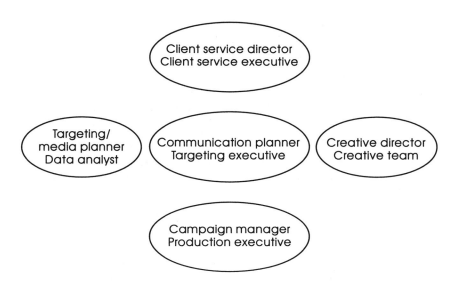

**Figure 9.4** Relationship marketing agency business team

organization and on business communication. The traditional marketing organization consists of marketing communication specialists arrayed opposite marketing management responsible for product communication (see Fig. 9.5).

Here no one owns the customer. Product or brand management may deliver different (and conflicting) messages to the same customer at the same time. Advertising, promotion or direct marketers may deliver different (and uncoordinated) messages with different themes. The process makes no sense to the customer.

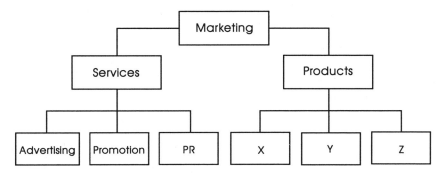

**Figure 9.5** Traditional marketing organization

Cross-selling opportunities are missed. Traditional organization wastes marketing money, and it is a barrier to any initiative designed to develop the customer.

In the new form of marketing organizations, communications will be run by generalists, and marketing managers will become customer relationship managers—responsible for the total customer relationship (see Fig. 9.6).

Relationship managers will be responsible for deployment of all organization resources to plan, to contact, and deliver to their customer segments. Business process engineering will develop new working practices to pull together in cross-functional teams, and to focus on customer service with marketing at the hub of each.

Customer relationship management can be the focus for the whole company—the banner to rally the troops. But the practice means the daily, nitty-gritty care for the customer. It means that everyone will have to work together. And it means that your front-line people are as important as your head office management. Ultimately the promise to the customer must be fulfilled wherever and whenever the customer deals with the company.

So relationship marketing is a starting-point for change. And feedback from the market-place should drive a re-engineering of the company and of its organization, to bring all the people closer to their customers.

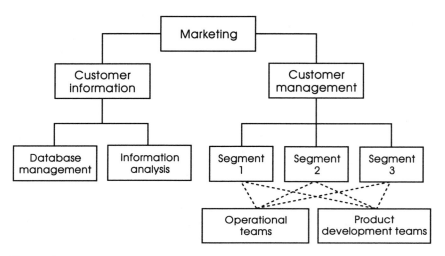

**Figure 9.6** Modern marketing organization

## Relationship marketing—and the barriers to change

The adoption of relationship marketing practice has been slow but steady. Growth has accelerated in Europe not only with recession but also with the fierce competition from the USA and Japan. There are still significant barriers to change.

The first barrier is *technological*. Investment is required in the resources required to manage relationship marketing. But new technology has resulted in a rapid fall in computing and telecommunication costs, bringing customer information systems down to desk-top PCs (Fig. 9.7). Customer systems are for the first time feasible and practicable propositions, and they can be managed directly by the marketing function.

The second barrier is *economic*. The real costs of reaching target audiences through mass media are escalating. Retail markets are becoming saturated, and salesforce costs are subject to sustained inflation. But falling costs in print, postage, and interactive, electronic media make direct communications and distribution increasingly attractive. Relationship marketing is for the first time a cost-effective proposition.

**Figure 9.7** Marketing workstation

The highest barriers are *cultural* and *educational*. Professionals trained in traditional marketing methods cannot but be wary of the new concept. Management faced with recession and competition cannot but be cautious about the investment. Businesses developed to deliver product to customer cannot but be challenged hugely by the prospect of becoming customer-driven.

Relationship marketing will demand enhanced skills in project planning and management, and higher levels of numeracy, as well as a deep understanding of interpersonal relationships. What matters is not what management says—but what the customer wants.

Relationship marketing requires new language and new tools. The business needs to think share of customer before share of market, and will need a new framework to plan and to evaluate marketing expenditure.

## Relationship marketing—and the financial pay-back

The objective of relationship marketing is to address and deliver directly to quantitative and qualitative business objectives.

Quantitatively, investments in customer relationships generate rapid pay-back and long-term revenue and profit streams. These processes of calculating and allocating the marketing budget can be modelled. Marketing expenditure should be treated as a business investment, and its allocation among different customer segments and different communication media and channels should be optimized, for maximum profitability (see Fig. 9.8).

When subject to this rigour most marketing functions will be pleasantly surprised that their budgets will rise. And most business management will be equally and pleasantly surprised to find themselves renewed advocates of the marketing cause.

Investments in customer relationships generate measurable improvements in customer satisfaction and retention rates—and (what is critical) in active customer loyalty. The great interest in customer satisfaction should not obscure the reality that this is a backward-looking measure. In relationship marketing we evaluate active loyalty, which looks forward to the potential future value of the customer.

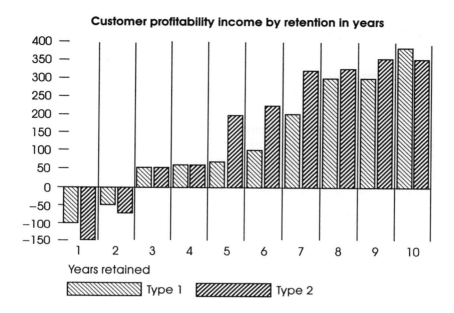

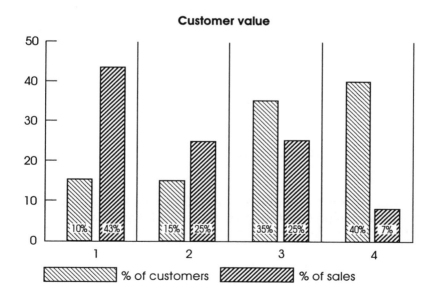

**Figure 9.8** Customer profitability and customer value

# Relationship marketing—and the quality of business

Relationship marketing also delivers qualitative benefits which enhance the quality of business through relationships both internal and external.

Ownership of customer information and customer relationships ensures the future by allowing the business a new degree of control. We can directly communicate to customers. We can observe their behaviour, listen to their signals, learn from their actions and address their concerns and needs.

Customers are people—not market share points, not faceless revenue streams. Relationship marketing simply fosters a better relationship between a business and its customers—a relationship based on a greater degree of open dialogue, mutual understanding and a basic level of honesty.

# Customer honesty test

Now test your own business for your customer honesty, with Stewart Pearson's four customer honesty tests:

1  Do you say thank you to customers?
2  Do you listen to your customers?
3  Do you learn more about your customers?
4  Do you compete aggressively for your customers?

# Checklist

Stewart Pearson's assertion that relationship marketing is the critical functional competence today, far exceeding in significance advertising or sales promotion, will raise a few eyebrows, particularly of those with vested interests in the more traditional forms of the communications mix. The special significance of relationship marketing is its focus on the individual customer as an individual, with unique needs or perceptions of needs. Within the orthodoxy of the marketing mix, the individual becomes a self-contained micro-segment and requires marketing focus at that level of precision. Direct marketing, in all the forms described by Stewart Pearson, certainly aspires to individual focus, particularly through personalization of the communications media, but the dilemma for all of us is to sustain the reality, or dare I say illusion, of individual values throughout the organization—at every point where the customer is impacted; accounts, after-sales-service, and operations, for example. Relationship marketing is fully integrated marketing and demands the culture of a marketing organization.

Stewart Pearson also argues with great conviction that we must be sensitive to the value potential of each customer and prospect. This powerful concept means that we must sign on to the notion of continuity rather than opportunism in our attitude to customers—hence his challenge to the world of sales promotion. In earlier chapters I have repeated the mantra that an existing customer is many times easier to sell to than a prospect, hence the need to invest time and effort in creating sufficient bonding to facilitate the continuity of sales.

This, as I have stressed, requires the management of the gaps between sales, as much as the sales pitch itself.

## Questions to consider

9.1  What are the potential uses for relationship marketing in our business?

9.2  What data do we have that allows us to identify customers as individuals?

9.3  What is the lifetime value potential of each customer?

9.4  What are the life-stages of customers that we can appeal to in particular?

9.5  What is the role for relationship marketing in business-to-business sales?

9.6  How do we store transactional history for each customer?

9.7  How able are we to analyse the transactional history of customers for indicators of future potential?

9.8  How well do we reward customer loyalty?

9.9  What do we do to promote customer loyalty?

9.10  What do we do to manage the gap between sales?

9.11  How well integrated are our business processes to ensure that the customer perceives coherent individual treatment?

9.12  How well do our information systems support relationship marketing?

9.13  How good are we at targeting only high potential prospects for specific offers?

9.14  How good are we at single-variable testing to establish the optimum offer?

**9.15** How consistent with our strategic aims are our tactical direct marketing campaigns?

**9.16** How supportive of brand development is our use of direct marketing?

**9.17** What measurement systems have we for establishing the effectiveness of our relationship management?

**9.18** What measurements ought we to have in place for relationship management?

**9.19** For business-to-business sales, what is the potential for direct marketing?

**9.20** What use could we make of direct marketing in developing relationships with influencers within the commercial customer's decision-making unit?

**9.21** What criteria should we use for managing the frequency and regularity of contact with existing customers or prospects?

**9.22** What are our ethical policies for telemarketing, direct mail and direct response advertising?

**9.23** Where will we find bench-mark standards of performance in relationship marketing?

**9.24** How well organized are we for integrated relationship management?

**9.25** How knowledgeable are we about the tools and techniques of relationship marketing so that we can brief suppliers to a professional standard?

Unlike many other aspects of the communications mix, relationship marketing makes particular demands on both suppliers—agencies, post office or distributors, mail shops, telemarketing agencies, geo-demographic systems, IT vendors and handling houses—and the marketing organization. No aspect of marketing is as scientific in its methodology or as demanding of disciplined systems for success. Because it can be deployed on a large scale it is perhaps easy to forget that its focus is always upon the individual—a critical success factor to be stressed internally and in all briefings to suppliers.

There can be no doubt, however, that relationship marketing will be the dominant theme for some time to come.

# 10

# Geodemographic segmentation

## You are where you live

### Richard Webber and Jim Hodgkins (CCN Marketing)

Segmentation is becoming an increasingly key issue for marketers as the focus of their activities shifts from macro to micro marketing. To market products and services effectively it is necessary not only to define and quantify a target audience but also to access information on the ability of localized media to reach it. The system that is used to do this must be robust, so that decisions can be made based on its findings. These decisions may vary from the location of outlets through to the selection of the audience that receives promotional literature.

Geodemographic modelling provides a valuable solution to businesses wishing to segment consumer markets. Whether the distribution channel is retail, mail order or through a field salesforce, for products from food to financial services, magazines to motor cars, geodemographic modelling is now used by most of the UK's larger consumer marketing organizations.

The assumption that underlies geodemographic modelling is that neighbourhoods attract similar sorts of people. If we can define a set of neighbourhood types that are broadly similar across a wide range of demographic indicators, then they are also likely to offer similar levels of opportunity for any widely advertised products or brands. These types are defined by statistically analysing a wide range of demographic measures for each neighbourhood in the country. The classification is independent, as all audiences, areas or lists of customers are analysed by the same classification. This avoids the problems that occur when different marketers describe customer characteristics using categories specific to their own application.

Geodemographic modelling allows marketers control through the provision of a data analysis system that enables much better understanding of customer and market characteristics. Applications have expanded greatly fuelled by the growth in application software, personal computer power and the demands of users.

Key benefits offered by classifying consumers in this way are as follows:

- *Coverage*  Every consumer in the county can be classified whether he or she is a customer, a respondent to a market research survey, a name and address on a mailing list or simply a person living in a particular area.
- *Flexibility*  The system can be used to link different types of data held on separate databases.
- *Convenience*  Coding data with the model is quick, easy and inexpensive. There is no need to interview people to find out their characteristics; their addresses are all that is needed to classify people.
- *Local detail*  Geodemographic modelling enables national research findings to be projected down to a very fine level of local detail enabling marketers to improve decision-making and achieve better results in all applications relating to local market segmentation.

This chapter explains how a geodemographic model is built, examines the applications of geodemographic models, gives a brief history of the discipline and looks at future trends.

## How geodemographic models are built

### Objective

The actual process of building a geodemographic model involves applying a range of statistical techniques to a vast quantity of spatially organized data. There are relatively few individuals or businesses in the UK with the training, resources and experience to enable them to build successful models. However, the ingredients and methods of building a system can be explained without excessive technical references.

Before examining the ingredients and method it is wise to look at the objective. What does a geodemographic model aim to achieve?

The main objective is to create a series of easy to interpret consumer types which each contain a reasonably homogenous population and that are as distinct as possible from each other. Separating the wealthy from the financially dependent, families from singles and young from old may appear a simple task. However, deciding precisely how best to combine information so as to produce an optimal set of consumer groups is not a simple process.

## Ingredients

Britain is a consumer market containing around 45 million adults in 23 million households. No two individuals are identical but characteristics can be identified that correlate highly with their behaviour. Of these characteristics demographic data supplied by the Office of Population and Census Statistics decennial census offers the largest available volume of information on a local area basis.

Demographic data are used in geodemographic modelling to infer likelihood to behave in a particular way, for example

- To own a particular product, e.g. a dishwasher
- To have a set of values or an attitude, e.g. voting preference
- To participate in an activity, e.g. playing bingo.

The census publishes counts for over 10 000 individual characteristics. However, the data are available only as statistical counts for neighbourhood areas, termed enumeration districts. These contain 180 households each, on average. Some geodemographic models use just these data while others supplement it with other data such as electoral roll information, data from the Postal Address File (PAF) and data held by credit reference agencies.

In all cases these data will be anonymized by creating statistics that relate to neighbourhoods. These will be either areas similar to the enumeration districts that the census data are released for or individual postcodes averaging 15 households each.

## Method

From all of the available data a series of statistical processes are used to discover which pieces of data are most predictive in measuring consumer behaviour.

The statistical process that all geodemographic models use is cluster analysis. It is clustering that creates the neighbourhood types that make up each system and give it an identity. Cluster codes will then be applied to all postcodes in an enumeration district, or if additional sources of data are used to each individual postcode.

Geodemographic models typically have a structure containing 30–60 distinct cluster types which are then grouped into 8–12 broader groups. Figure 10.1 illustrates the MOSAIC geodemographic model.

| Groups | Types | Description |
|---|---|---|
| L1 High income families → L1 | High income families | 1   Clever capitalists |
| L2 Suburban semis | 1   Clever capitalists → | |
| L3 Blue-collar owners | 2   Rising materialists | Clever captalists are typically wealthy people involved in |
| L4 Low rise council | 3   Corporate careerists | management of companies and in |
| L5 Council flats | 4   Ageing professionals | broking, commercial |
| L6 Victorian low status | 5   Small-time business | trading, importing and |
| L7 Town houses and flats | | exporting |
| L8 Stylish singles | | The areas are characterized by |
| L9 Independent elders | | company directors living in large detached |
| L10 Mortgaged families | | houses, though not necessarily with |
| L11 Country dwellers | | extensive grounds, in well-established |
| L12 Institutional areas | | residential areas within reasonable reach of city centres |
| | | Children are typically of secondary school age or students and there is a higher proportion of foreigners than in the more suburban types within high income families |

**Figure 10.1** Structure of geodemographic system illustrated by MOSAIC
*Source*: CCN Marketing MOSAIC database 1993

The model is then adapted to the applications discussed in the next section in two forms, as a postcode directory for appending codes to name and address files and as a database containing the number and proportion of households and population falling within each code for each neighbourhood. However, a critical factor in the growth of geodemographic modelling is that software modules for analysing areas and individuals, reporting on them and mapping them are an integral part of the geodemographic solution. Figure 10.2 illustrates how the various components of a geodemographic software and data system combine.

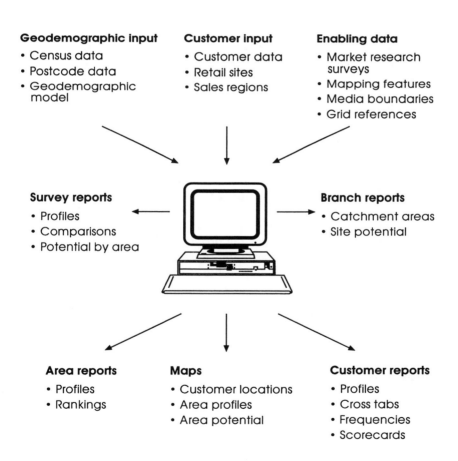

**Geodemographic input**
- Census data
- Postcode data
- Geodemographic model

**Customer input**
- Customer data
- Retail sites
- Sales regions

**Enabling data**
- Market research surveys
- Mapping features
- Media boundaries
- Grid references

**Survey reports**
- Profiles
- Comparisons
- Potential by area

**Branch reports**
- Catchment areas
- Site potential

**Area reports**
- Profiles
- Rankings

**Maps**
- Customer locations
- Area profiles
- Area potential

**Customer reports**
- Profiles
- Cross tabs
- Frequencies
- Scorecards

**Figure 10.2** Configuration of a geodemographic software and data solution

# Geodemographic applications

This section describes implementing geodemographic modelling within your business to help improve performance. It explains what a geodemographic profile is and how it can be combined with other data and systems to achieve marketing advantage. Examples are based on the MOSAIC geodemographic model.

## Profiling

In all applications profiling is used to provide an objective analysis of a product, medium or area. Having examined the way that geodemographic models are built it is necessary to understand how profiling works. It is a simple method for comparing the distributions by MOSAIC of two different sets of data. The first set, the target, is commonly the MOSAIC distribution of customer addresses, responses to a question on a research survey or a geographic area. The second set is the base for comparison. In a simple profiling exercise this may be the MOSAIC distribution of all adults or all households in Britain or, in the case of a research study, it may be the MOSAIC distribution of all respondents. However, the decision of which base to use is an important one as it affects the results greatly.

Table 10.1 shows a profile of all credit card owners against a base of all households. It has been obtained from the Target Group Index market research survey. The geographic model shown is MOSAIC, which has 12 Groups and 52 types; only the Group level data are shown in the table. Looking at the profile in Table 10.1 it is easy to see that credit card owners are over represented in particular groups. What makes geodemographic modelling so important is the ability to develop actionable marketing programmes from these data. There are three main areas of implementation of geodemographic models which cover between them many applications of data in marketing. These are planning and research, database marketing, and customer acquisition.

## Planning and research

### Market research

Geodemographic models can be used to build structured sample frames for market research purposes. When postal, doorstep or telephone research is to be undertaken the identification of neighbourhoods and individual households which meet the required criteria for interviewing can save survey costs.

**Table 10.1** Profile of credit card owners

| MOSAIC Group | | Credit card owners[a] (%) | Adults (GB)[b] (%) | Adults with a credit card[c] (%) | Index[d] (GB = 100) |
|---|---|---|---|---|---|
| L1 | High income families | 15.96 | 11.23 | 61.0 | 143 |
| L2 | Suburban semis | 16.32 | 12.93 | 54.2 | 127 |
| L3 | Blue-collar owners | 15.75 | 16.03 | 42.2 | 99 |
| L4 | Low rise council | 9.67 | 16.43 | 25.3 | 59 |
| L5 | Council flats | 2.41 | 4.94 | 21.0 | 49 |
| L6 | Victorian low status | 7.03 | 8.49 | 35.5 | 83 |
| L7 | Town houses and flats | 10.96 | 10.48 | 42.9 | 100 |
| L8 | Stylish singles | 4.35 | 3.68 | 50.6 | 118 |
| L9 | Independent elders | 5.27 | 4.97 | 45.6 | 107 |
| L10 | Mortgaged families | 5.27 | 4.40 | 51.4 | 120 |
| L11 | Country dwellers | 6.72 | 5.67 | 50.9 | 119 |
| L12 | Institutional areas | 0.27 | 0.23 | 49.0 | 115 |
| | | 100 | 100 | 42.7 | 100 |

*Source*: TGI (Target Group Index—a quarterly consumer survey available by subscription only).
*Notes:*
[a]Credit card owners gives the percentage of all credit card owners that fall within the MOSAIC Group. The sum is 100% as all cardholders have been allocated to a group.
[b]Adults (GB) gives the percentage of all British adults that are in the MOSAIC Group. Again this column sums to 100.
[c]Adults with a credit card states the percentage of adults that are credit card owners. The figure of 42.7% for each group is the average for Britain.
[d]Index shows the extent to which each MOSAIC Group is under or over represented compared to the national average. L1 High income families has an index 143 meaning that there are 1.43 times the national average representation of High income families among credit card owners.

Geodemographic models are frequently used to analyse *ad hoc* or syndicated research surveys enabling marketers to identify the types of areas in which concentrations of particular types of individuals live.

Potential buyers of new products can be identified and profiled by a geodemographic model and their geographical distribution examined, enabling the best test markets and outlets to be identified.

Local media owners wishing to improve their professionalism of display advertising presentations often use geodemographic profiles of their distribution areas to show the suitability of their title for the target group of the advertisers whose budget they are bidding for.

It is the combination of the client's information with geodemographic data that enables an effective solution to be produced.

### Network planning

Major companies with networks of stores, branches, restaurants, franchises or direct salesforces use geodemographic models to improve the location of their outlets and to adapt concepts and merchandise to the requirements of the local communities that they serve.

Geodemographic data are often combined with other data for analysing and forecasting. For example a bank wishing to change the profile of its branches by appointing specialist consultants in selected branches to sell mortgages and retirement planning may appoint a geodemographic modelling company to

- Analyse what types of people buy these services.
- Assign a market opportunity value to each branch in the network for each type of specialist.
- Suggest the best sites for locating new branches containing these specialists.

The analysis will involve

- Using customer data to calculate the outer limits of branch catchment areas.
- Using customer and research survey data to determine the profile and spend of buyers within that area.
- Calculating total potential for each branch catchment.
- Creating a model to analyse market share, by examining local competition.

- Producing a management report and detailed statistical reports advising the results.
- Providing an in-house system for producing 'what if' models for a range of scenarios.

## Database marketing

The use of geodemographic modelling in database marketing depends greatly on the volume and relevance of the data held on all individuals on the database.

The geodemographic codes are frequently used for the following purposes:

- Examining the differences between customers buying different products and services.
- Analysing changes over time in the composition of new customers.
- Finding groups of customers that are best suited to the cross-selling of different products.
- Analysing customer spend, profitability, bad debt, stability and payment methods.
- Examining the difference between the profiles of customers of different branches.
- Analysing the response to promotional campaigns of customers on the database.

An example of database analysis over time is shown in Table 10.2 using data on credit card owners.

A credit card company wishes to analyse who is currently applying for credit cards to estimate future spend patterns. It takes data on those who have taken out a card in the last 12 months and compares this to all owners of credit cards. From the profile in Table 10.2 it can be seen that Group L8 Stylish singles has the greatest penetration of applicants and the highest index although in Table 10.1 it was ranked only fifth for credit card ownership. This change in the customer database will affect the marketing strategy immediately. It may also affect the volume of spend on cards, the types of products purchased using them and the expenditure on credit cards at different types of outlets. Over time this will have great impact on the credit card operator's turnover and profitability.

With databases that contain little detail about each individual the geodemographic codes are a vital analysis and selection tool. On databases where large volumes of customer data are held, including

**Table 10.2** Database analysis over time of credit card owners

| MOSAIC Group | | Acquired credit card last 12 mths[a] (%) | Credit card owners[b] (%) | Penetration of credit card[c] (%) | Index[d] |
|---|---|---|---|---|---|
| L1 | High income families | 17.48 | 15.96 | 5.6 | 110 |
| L2 | Suburban semis | 14.72 | 16.32 | 4.1 | 91 |
| L3 | Blue-collar owners | 15.19 | 15.75 | 3.4 | 97 |
| L4 | Low rise council | 8.41 | 9.67 | 1.8 | 89 |
| L5 | Council flats | 1.50 | 2.91 | 1.1 | 63 |
| L6 | Victorian low status | 8.70 | 7.03 | 3.7 | 125 |
| L7 | Town houses and flats | 9.35 | 10.96 | 3.1 | 86 |
| L8 | Stylish singles | 6.15 | 4.35 | 6.0 | 143 |
| L9 | Independent elders | 4.58 | 5.27 | 3.3 | 87 |
| L10 | Mortgaged families | 6.67 | 5.27 | 5.5 | 128 |
| L11 | Country dwellers | 6.94 | 6.72 | 4.4 | 104 |
| L12 | Institutional areas | 0.23 | 0.27 | 3.0 | 88 |
| | | 100 | 100 | 3.5 | |

*Source:* TGI (Target Group Index—a quarterly consumer survey available by subscription only).
[a]Acquired credit card last 12 months gives the percentage of recent successful applicants that fall within the MOSAIC Group. The sum is 100% as all new card holders have been allocated to a group.
[b]Credit card owners gives the percentage of all credit card owners that are in the MOSAIC Group. Again this column sums to 100.
[c]Penetration of credit card states the percentage of adults that have acquired a credit card in the last 12 months. The figure of 3.5% for each group is the average for Britain.
[d]Index shows the extent to which each MOSAIC Group is under or over represented among recent credit card acquirers compared to all credit card owners.

individual demographic characteristics such as age, length of residence, marital status, home ownership and income, the codes are most useful for two purposes. First, they provide a quick analysis of any set of individuals, and second, they enable database information to be used for purposes such as research and planning and customer acquisition modelling.

## Customer acquisition

Geodemographic models are regularly used to improve the cost effectiveness of customer acquisition using direct mail and door-to-door leaflet distribution. They are also increasingly being applied to media selection for print and broadcast media and poster sites.

### Direct mail

Using the geodemographic profile, names and addresses can be selected which are in the types that have the highest indices on a profile. Many local promotions such as store openings, leisure events, home improvement offers, product launches and charity fund raising use this approach.

National advertisers usually organize local campaigns centrally and geodemographic modelling gives centralized marketing departments the ability to accurately analyse local market characteristics that they are not familiar with.

Geodemographic models are also used in more complex selections often involving the use of multiple regression models to select the best individuals to mail using a wide range of data combining geodemographic models with the data available on electoral register based lists enables the more accurate selection of prospects. Other factors analysed often include an individual's gender, household structure, length of residence, likely age (estimated from electoral register information) and their credit profile.

### Leaflet distribution

Most of the country's leading door-to-door distributors now use MOSAIC applications software to improve the level of targeting they offer their customers. Having MOSAIC-profiled each of their distribution blocks, the companies match their users' products to the profiles of their distribution areas so as to restrict distribution to areas where there is likely to be product demand.

Table 10.3 shows a ranking of all the postcode sectors in a store catchment by their potential to buy. The marketing manager can

**Table 10.3** Brick ranking report by postcode sectors

Zone Name: Guildford
Target: High Income Families
Base: Total households

| Rank Brick | Brick description | Target | Base | Penetration | Index |
|---|---|---|---|---|---|
| 1 KT24 6 | West Horsley | 737 | 1499 | 0.492 | 216 *** |
| 2 GU 1 2 | Merrow | 1723 | 3833 | 0.450 | 197 ** |
| 3 GU 4 8 | Shalford | 785 | 2095 | 0.375 | 164 ** |
| 4 GU 3 1 | Compton | 269 | 726 | 0.371 | 163 ** |
| 5 GU 4 7 | Bushy Hill | 1333 | 3805 | 0.350 | 154 ** |
| 6 KT24 5 | Effingham | 515 | 1809 | 0.285 | 125 ** |
| 7 GU 2 5 | Guildford Park | 987 | 3971 | 0.249 | 109 |
| 8 GU 5 0 | Bramley | 574 | 2404 | 0.239 | 105 |
| 9 GU 3 3 | Worplesdon | 458 | 1998 | 0.229 | 101 |
| 10 GU 1 3 | Epsom Rd | 330 | 1666 | 0.198 | 87 |
| 11 GU 5 9 | Gomshall | 203 | 1448 | 0.140 | 62 – – |
| 12 GU 1 1 | Bellfields | 575 | 4202 | 0.137 | 60 – – |
| 13 GU 2 6 | Stoughton | 304 | 6880 | 0.044 | 19 – – – |
| 14 GU 1 4 | North St | 1 | 2257 | 0.000 | 0 – – – |
| Zone total | | 8794. | 38593. | 0.228 | |

© CCN Marketing, Talbot House, Talbot Street, Nottingham NG1 5HF
Tel: 0115 9410888 Fax: 0115 9344903
Source: CCN Marketing MOSAIC database 1993
Note: Brick = level of geographic area analysed, in this case postal sector

decide to prioritize sectors to deliver a certain volume of leaflets or to distribute to all areas where potential is above a given limit.

**Print and broadcast**

Local media such as regional newspapers and independent local radio are often prioritized using a similar ranking to that shown for leaflet distribution. The areas analysed in this case are broadcast coverage areas rather than postal sectors.

National media profiles can be matched to those of products to show which titles offer the best sales opportunity (see Table 10.4).

# History and trends in geodemographic modelling

The first commercial application of geodemographic modelling in Britain was in 1977 when the British Market Research Bureau

**Table 10.4** Ranking of national daily newspaper titles by their similarity to the profile of Volvo car buyers

| Newspaper | Match index (AV = 100) |
|---|---|
| *Daily Telegraph* | 133 |
| *The Times* | 126 |
| *The Independent* | 115 |
| *Daily Mail* | 113 |
| *Daily Express* | 109 |
| *Guardian* | 104 |
| *Today* | 101 |
| *Daily Record* | 85 |
| *Daily Mirror* | 84 |
| *The Sun* | 84 |
| *The Star* | 77 |

*Source*: TGI (Target Group Index—a quarterly consumer survey available by subscription only).

(BMRB) used CRN (Classification of Residential Neighbourhood), a ward parish classification, to improve the representativeness of their Target Group Index (TGI) survey. When analysing product and media fields on the TGI by CRN, Ken Baker and John Bermingham (1979) of BMRB discovered that geodemographic data were more effective discriminators of readership of the *Guardian* and *Daily Telegraph* than the most commonly used indicators of status such as social class.

In 1980 an American consultancy, CACI, adopted the system, which had originally been built for public sector analysis of areas of deprivation, rebranded it ACORN (A Classification Of Residential Neighbourhoods) and sold it as a system for analysing the potential of retail sites.

In 1981 the system was linked to all postcodes enabling the coding of geographic areas, the TGI and of customer files by direct marketers. The ACORN codes were also added to the electoral register belonging to CCN Systems, part of Great Universal Stores, and used to select mailing lists which provided commercially worthwhile response rates.

The number of classifications expanded following the release of 1981 census data and in 1986 CCN Systems launched its own classification, MOSAIC, which was the first to use significant volumes of data from sources other than the census.

In the late eighties the systems on offer included PIN from Pinpoint Analysis, Super Profiles from CDMS, Define from Infolink as well as ACORN and MOSAIC.

Important advances that aided the expansion of geodemographics included the growth of direct mail volumes, with a requirement for targeting names and addresses, and the dramatic fall in the costs of computer processing.

Geodemographic suppliers now offer PC systems in which to run customer and geodemographic data and CCN Marketing and CACI are the main suppliers with around 300 installations in Britain.

The use of other data in the PC systems, particularly that generated from mass consumer surveys such as the National Shopper Survey by CMT Ltd, is a trend which is likely to continue in the nineties. Marketers require more detail about buying patterns and, now that profitable methods of distributing questionnaires containing over 100 questions that generate up to 1 million responses annually have been achieved, marketers can satisfy this need.

Within the core discipline of geodemographic modelling trends in the mid-nineties include

- Extension of geodemographics into other European markets and the construction of pan-European segmentation systems such as EURO-MOSAIC.
- Building models to suit individual markets such as Financial MOSAIC and Investor ACORN.
- Creating more detailed models for areas within Britain such as Scotland and London.

The growth of geodemographic modelling and the market analysis business is strong and the only cloud on the horizon is the threat of control on the use and application of certain types of data by the Data Protection Registrar in Britain and the European Union.

During the nineties it is our expectation that the growth of micro marketing will intensify the use of market analysis and databased marketing and that software tools will satisfy an ever widening range of applications with the marketing departments of British and European companies.

# Checklist

In a perfect world marketers would communicate only with prospects they know are going to buy—no risk, no waste and no brickbats. In the less than perfect world we inhabit how close to perfection can we get? What prospect to sale ratio would we regard as satisfactory? The answer will vary with the sector being considered and the offering, but the principle holds good, whether we think of multi-million pound capital investment projects or circulation of a daily paper, that we should seek to communicate only with high propensity prospects and avoid promoting those who would, almost certainly, never buy. Marketing budgets are, after all, finite: it makes sense to use it to maximum effect on the prospect base most likely to respond.

Richard Webber and Jim Hodgkins have described the logical and experiential basis for MOSAIC and its derivatives and have demonstrated that the correlative links between one or more types of activities and a propensity to buy something else are commonly high. While geodemographics may have started as a housing-based classification system, we are today dealing with very powerful regression analyses of millions of purchase transactions in almost every sector of consumer expenditure. This is the key to understanding: we are able to add the prior behavioural history of prospects to behaviours we have observed from our own transactional experience. We have access to lifestyle indicators rather than the narrower focus of our own sector.

This ability to target more cost-effectively is the financial pay-back. The greater prize comes from being better able to understand what makes our customers tick and how best to stimulate them. As geodemographics grows in international markets the ability to achieve large savings on brand development and general marketing communications becomes obvious. However, the subject is highly specialized and, like direct marketing in all its forms, repays very careful study. There are few specialists in the market, so it is wise to use only the leading firms in the field which besides CCN include CACI and CDMS. Geodemographics are one of the most potent tools available to the consumer marketer and, like all toxic remedies, they need to be handled with care.

## Questions to consider

**10.1**   How confident are we that our distribution network is appropriate for the real distribution of our end-users?

**10.2**  When did we last check this distribution pattern out?

**10.3**  What are the criteria we use for geographic marketing?

**10.4**  How effective are we at geographic analysis of our markets?

**10.5**  What would the benefit be of being able to conduct market research at micro-segment level rather than macro?

**10.6**  What do we believe the correlative lifestyle factors are in our customer buying motivations?

**10.7**  How might we establish those correlative links?

**10.8**  What is our current prospect to customer ratio?

**10.9**  What difference would it make to our cost-of-sale if the prospect/customer ratio were improved?

**10.10**  What are the underlying demographic trends in the markets we serve?

**10.11**  What are the demographic trends in the lifestage segments we serve?

**10.12**  What correlation is there between credit score and geographic location?

**10.13**  What impact could geodemographics have on media targeting to prospect markets?

**10.14**  What do we have to do to our customer records to be able to profile them using MOSAIC or comparable systems?

**10.15**  What are the key indicators in our customer behaviour we wish to analyse for their significance?

**10.16**  How might we segment our customers differently using systems like MOSAIC?

**10.17**  How might we test geodemographic profiling?

**10.18**  What part does direct marketing play in our customer strategy?

**10.19**  In what ways do mail-order customers differ from retail customers?

**10.20**  What else do our prospects and customers do with their disposable income?

**10.21**  What other marketing organization might we collaborate with in promoting to prospects we both value?

**10.22**  What added-value services and products could we add to our range as a result of geodemographic profiling?

**10.23**  What market segments, revealed through geodemographic profiling, might represent attractive potential markets for strategic investment?

**10.24**  What is our definition of the ideal prospect or customer?

**10.25**  How will we integrate geodemographic profiling with our market research, direct marketing, product development and marketing communications processes?

Those organizations who have substantial consumer markets will, without doubt, acquire significant competitive advantage from systems like MOSAIC, ACORN, *et al.*—the ability to focus the marketing effort and to be more certain that hidden markets are not being ignored, are large prizes. The relationship between geodemographics and other aspects of the marketing tool-set is of prime importance today—it will be one of the critical competences for marketers in the near future.

# 11

# Telemarketing

## Getting ever closer to home

### Wendy Aldiss (Inbound Outbound)

Telebusiness is a more appropriate term than telemarketing for most companies today. Telebusiness can be defined as any part of a company's business which is carried out primarily over the telephone in a way that is planned and controlled, and which is designed to open up lines of communication between a company and its customers or prospects and to give or gather information. Telephone marketing (telemarketing) has attracted a somewhat limiting definition as the telebusiness executed solely as part of a marketing strategy.

Telemarketing started in the USA, which enjoys a far more innovative business culture than the UK. Among some of the earliest users were the Ford Motor Company and Coca Cola, who saw the potential value of making outbound calls. So successful have the telebusiness innovations been in the USA that they have been gradually adopted in the UK albeit with certain essential adaptations to suit the British market-place. Germany and France have also followed the US example, and gradually the rest of Europe, then the rest of the developed world. Japan is a keen user too.

As the costs of other sales and marketing tools have grown, so telephone usage has increased. It is generally accepted that telemarketing agencies alone generate revenue of around £75 million each year in the UK.

Like all telebusiness procedures, telemarketing enables person-to-person communication on a small or mass scale. It is an extraordinarily powerful marketing tool. Comparing telemarketing to most other marketing methods is like comparing a laser beam to torchlight.

Advertising, however good the research it is based on, is essentially a broadcasting media: ads send out your message to a wider audience, but the communication is only one way, transitory and shallow. Because telemarketing relies upon two-way communication with each person, it enables you to penetrate and exploit your market by creating a personal interface—the most personal interface you can have short of meeting your target in the flesh.

## Uses of telemarketing

Typically, telemarketing is used for

- Taking requests for company literature
- Taking, creating and upgrading orders
- Customer care
- Service calls
- Customer retention
- Increasing loyalty
- Making appointments
- Introducing new services or products
- Encouraging people to attend events.

All the above telemarketing activities enhance your marketing mix by bringing you closer to the customer.

Part of the secret of telemarketing's power, the element that elevates it above other ingredients in the marketing mix, is its singular ability to create a one-to-one relationship with a customer or prospect. It makes the connection that lies at the very heart of all business—the dialogue between buyer and seller.

Let us follow, for example, Acme Ltd, a fictitious company considering launching a new product. Enjoying a healthy cash flow it wishes to increase its range of goods or services. An idea for a new product has been kicking around for some time. But how big a demand for it is there?

Market research begins: conversations, conducted either on the telephone or in the flesh, with people either individually or in groups. The feedback is good. A few sample designs are produced and reaction is tested, again on a one-to-one or group basis. The results are positive. The money is there, the demand is there, and production and supply pose no problems. The signal is given. Lights turn to green and minds turn to the launch.

Having scrutinized the market research, creative teams begin designing the advertising. Which publications? Where in the publication will it attract most attention? At what price? What about mailshots? Coupons? Trial packs?

It is at around this time that Acme Ltd says 'goodbye' to the responses of individuals and 'hello' to what it perceives is the market. Computer predictions take precedence over research reports. Reality is replaced by virtual reality. Certainly, Acme's marketing is slick and professional and based on accurate research, but it acts like a blanket; while intending to cover the market the company has inadvertently smothered its voice. Acme's direct marketing will yield a response rate of around 3 per cent; the remaining 97 per cent will remain silent. It is a poor reward.

The additions of two telemarketing practices to the marketing mix could make all the difference and ensure that the investment in time, effort and money yields its full potential.

## Dedicated telephone numbers

First, by including a dedicated telephone number in its marketing output, Acme Ltd could easily begin re-establishing the individual link with its customers that it enjoyed during its fruitful days of market research. It will gain more responses, from those people who would not normally write but will phone; in addition it can impress its customers or prospect in a way that no mass-produced letter (however carefully worded) can.

Through telemarketing, Acme can project an image of caring professionalism, while finding out much more information about its market. It can find out why people responded; if they have used a similar product or not; how suitable it is; whether they usually use a competitor's product; how easy it is to buy; how much they spend on the product per year; how often they make that purchase. Ask the right questions and listen to the answers.

Telemarketing also lets Acme introduce the customer or prospect to other lines which the call reveals are relevant to their needs— something it would never know by simply putting things in the post or on the page of a journal.

## Non-responders and lost subscribers

Second, outbound telemarketing made to a selection or all of the non-responders (subject to industry restrictions) will establish why this percentage remained silent, convert some to customers and point the way forward towards more effective marketing in the future.

Not only is telemarketing a powerful medium in its own right and when enhancing the effectiveness of other aspects of marketing but also, unlike some other ingredients you find in the mix, telemarketing is a friendly medium. It combines well with the other ingredients and can either lead or support them in creating a successful strategy. In fact, so dependent has marketing become on the telebusiness that if you take the telephone out of market research, or erase the freephone number from the above-the-line advertising (to give just two examples) you would seriously impair many marketing strategies.

So the question when to use telemarketing is almost academic: you are probably already using it and have been doing so for years. In short, you could use telemarketing whenever it is advantageous and cost effective to have controlled and planned one-to-one communication with a targeted audience.

One true success story involves a company who used the telephone to lower attrition. This finance organization decreased their attrition rate by 70 per cent by making a single phone call to selected subscribers. They were already doing regular communication mailings, encouraging members to use their product more, some with incentives. They undertook a lot of market research to keep in touch with their members and to find out what they wanted in terms of new services. They were very proactive, conscientious in providing what they knew their general member profile wanted. Yet it was when they introduced telephone calls, carried out three months prior to the date when the subscription was due, that attrition dropped by 70 per cent. Through the calls they could provide what the individual member wanted.

## Care lines

Care lines generate customer feedback and brand loyalty. In the USA 83 per cent of FMCG (fast-moving consumer goods) products carry a care line number. Companies are well aware that if a problem arises within the company and it is dealt with in a positive way, even if it is not totally solved, the customer can be converted to be an advocate of the company. Left unsolved a bad image spreads very quickly. Telebusiness can be used to raise your company's profile or to reinforce product awareness. Certain activities will be performed on an ongoing basis, year in, year out; others tactically. While the instances where you should use telebusiness would fill an entire book, it would not be wise to use telebusiness when it is not cost effective.

The difficulty with defining the cost efficiency of telebusiness is that there is so much you achieve through the telephone that it is hard to quantify. For example, if you run a customer service department it is difficult to tell on a week-by-week, month-by-month basis what sort of additional loyalty you are building up with your customers which itself will increase sales. Even in instances where telemarketing is, at first glance, clearly inappropriate, it may have a role to play later in the sales cycle. For example, telemarketing cannot be used where your sales team have to physically be there to see the stocks on a shelf or the physical environment of a company. However, it could be used to maintain contact between personal visits or as an inbound facility for additional orders to be placed. It is ideal to bridge gaps in sales territories.

Some people are still wary of making commitment over the phone and need a personal visit. These can, however, be arranged and followed up by phone. Standards of service and/or delivery can be monitored through phone calls.

## Thoroughness and versatility

It is known that telemarketing can increase the size and detail of the response from the usual direct marketing mailshot, but it has many more strengths than that. By its very nature—being a planned and controlled exercise in one-to-one communication—it can replicate the function of a personal visit from your company's representative, which is an increasingly expensive exercise and not always the best way of dealing with the client or customer.

Probably most salespeople would find it hard to maintain a rate of five appointments per day. A good telemarketer should make contact with around five decision-makers *per hour*, and will face less risk of initial rejection. How many sales are lost in face-to-face meetings because of some prejudice on the part of the customer? It does not happen on the telephone. Not only is each call tailored to the objective but also a good telemarketer becomes just the type of person that the customer on the other end of the phone wants them to be.

## Flexibility and immediacy

To the qualities of thoroughness and versatility we can add a third: flexibility. Let us suppose that something happens in your market-place that needs an immediate response. You probably cannot afford to put out a new television campaign or intercept your direct mail deliveries nor to recall your salespeople from the field, retrain them, then send them out again in the space of a few hours. But you can change the wording of your phone calls and start spreading the message almost straight away. No other marketing medium lets you do this.

This flexibility allows you to improve your own performance as well. Perhaps you have started with a style of approach that works, but as time goes on it becomes inappropriate. (You can tell by monitoring the success of the calls when or where something is going wrong.) With telemarketing you can simply change the presentation—easily, cheaply, effectively, immediately.

This leads us to the fourth and probably the most important contribution that telebusiness will make to your marketing mix. Telebusiness will make you think more deeply about the objectives, structure, expectations and results of the campaign than any other method because of the immediacy of its response. Once you have opened up a phone line to your customers or prospects—inbound or outbound, it does not matter which—you will not be able to avoid hearing both their opinion of you and their real requirements. A company may advertise an 0800 prefix telephone number, offering a particular car or software bargain in the belief that this will form the sole topic of conversation. Some hope! They will get everything, and they will start learning very fast exactly what their customers think of them. So telebusiness should force you to think about the whole business you are in and you should be prepared to take that on board.

## Advantages of telebusiness

Is this an advantage or a disadvantage? I firmly believe that the company who makes itself accessible in this manner—through planned, controlled professionally executed telebusiness—holds a permanent and distinct advantage over those of its competitors who are not using telebusiness. If you open up a customer services line, that will be the number where your customers know that they can get a decent response; where they will always be listened to; where something will always be done. No other form of marketing has the same ability to give customers and prospects the feeling that their complaints or suggestions will be followed through so well or that the company is on their side.

This concept of being accessible and friendly to the customer is still alien to too many companies in the UK who continue to prefer the brutal certainties of operating as hunters and gatherers, rather than putting the extra effort required into cultivating their customers. Their primitive view of the customer begins and ends with a quick kill at the point and moment of sale. Quite frankly, once they have taken the cash, they lose interest in the customer; or worse, the customer is regarded as trouble and brushed off. Why this should be is unclear, especially in the light of the American business experience. Perhaps it is just another example of the difference between the more open manner in the USA and the chillier, more reserved way that such matters are dealt with in the UK.

## Disadvantages of telebusiness

Naturally, telebusiness has what for some people will appear to be drawbacks. Professional telebusiness is not easy and it does not come cheap. You have to have the right environment, expensive equipment, all the staff overheads and, above all, be prepared to pay for professional training. Badly performed telebusiness will be seriously damaging to your company's health. We have already seen how telebusiness makes you look long and hard at your marketing basics. There is no short-cut to good telebusiness: you have to take it step by step. It is like any other marketing campaign: if you do not sit down and target your people properly, design your creative approach and think what you are trying to achieve, you will not achieve half the results that you could have expected if you had planned well.

If you choose to use an external resource, you have to put just as much thought and planning into what you are trying to achieve—if not more—than if you are doing it in-house.

## Tailoring outbound calls

It is quite possible that for your company to get value for money from telebusiness and enjoy the benefits outlined above, certain corporate attitudes will have to change. All your calls—inbound or outbound—must be handled professionally by well-trained staff using suitable telephony and working to achievable and cost-effective targets.

Outbound calls should be carefully tailored to each particular customer or prospect. Their form and content merit serious thought. It should be obvious to companies (but often it is not) that a good call guide is more than just a replication of the same words you might use when meeting customers face-to-face, or in a brochure. Telephone communication is just not like that. Besides ensuring fluency, a well-written call guide means you can handle a wide variety of attitudes. Even if your customers or prospects say that they are not interested because their budget does not come up for review for another six months, it is not just a 'No'. It is an indication that in four months' time it is worth ringing the customer. So, whereas from direct marketing you had only a 3 per cent response and the remaining 97 per cent you know nothing about, with telemarketing, even if you increase response by only 5 per cent on the first call you know *why* the other people are saying 'No'. You define the people who said 'No' into different types of 'No' and communicate with them again at the optimum time, with a history of contact and exactly the right message for that person.

## Handling inbound calls

For some companies, *maximizing value* means reducing the costs of calls to a minimum, often by shortening inbound calls in a frenzied bid to increase productivity with little thought for what you or the caller are gaining. I would argue for a more sophisticated balance and prefer to think in terms of optimum cost for the maximum return.

Why have so many inbound call centres concentrated their attention on shifting inbound calls as fast as they can? Because they do not want to keep people waiting? Well, if they employ a few more staff they will not have to keep people waiting. But, you might argue, that puts up the cost of the operation. Okay, well let us see what a company stands to gain from those calls if a bit more time is spent on them.

Take the example of someone ringing up and asking for a particular holiday which is already fully booked. What would the usual response be?

'I'm sorry. That holiday is fully booked now. Thank you for calling. Goodbye.'

Excellent. The telemarketer has got rid of the customer quickly and reasonably politely. Call duration was within target. Everyone is happy. But how about, when the customer is on the phone showing an interest in a product, the company representative —for that is what the telemarketer is—shows some interest in the customer and suggests another date or another destination, which may be just as viable for the customer. They may make a sale. Is it not worth employing an extra person to take the calls that were not answered because they were taking the time to deal with calls in this way? A sale has been made and the company may have gained a loyal customer. Loyal or not, the customer has not gone to a competitor who may bother to take the time.

Always bear in mind how much pressure you are putting staff under to get rid of calls the minute they are answered. Staff absenteeism and turnover are themselves a cost. Maximizing the value of each call means attaining the correct balance between costs and the results you get as a business.

## Future of telebusiness

As to the future of telebusiness, I believe that it will be in increasingly common use in a widening variety of business ventures. Like every other product of the revolution in information technology, telebusiness systems will become simultaneously more sophisticated and simpler to use, as well as cheaper to buy and more widely available. Progress is doing more with less.

Already many companies have their telephone departments linked to their distribution system. The moment an item request is keyed in, it is automatically sent to the distribution department and the item is sent out that night. Soon database and script package will include background data, allowing calls to be automatically diaried forward to a particular time, based on past analysis, receipt of stock, discounted prices, etc.

As geodemographics and other modelling software becomes more widely available, we shall be able to get the systems to alter the scripts and improve prompts to telebusiness users. Businesses in the financial sector will have calls triggered automatically by customer behaviour. When the customer does something, such as buying some shares or going overdrawn, the system will place them in a queue for the telebusiness person, complete with the appropriate call guide.

Figures are deplorably scarce, but the most recent survey indicates that in 1992 the telebusiness spend in UK companies with over 100 employees stood at £10.4 billion (Henley Centre Telebusiness Survey, 1994). As impressive as this figure is, I would suggest that if companies continue to develop telebusiness creatively, the increase in its use will be dramatic. After all, telebusiness has the potential to reach out to even more of the adult population.

I am a committed advocate of professional telebusiness because I have seen just how effective it can be. Frankly, a lot of current practice is terribly mediocre. You do not have to make vast adjustments to see a tremendous improvement. In today's competitive world, where many companies are often distinguishable from their competitors only through their reputation for quality of service, telebusiness should be giving your marketing mix the edge that will allow you to capture and keep your competitor's customers.

## Checklist

Telemarketing, or telebusiness as Wendy Aldiss urges us to call it, is big business worldwide and getting bigger by the minute. Is this rational? Or is it, perhaps, a symptom of everyone jumping on the latest bandwagon, all else in marketing communications having (presumably) failed?

The forensic marketer will have no ambiguity about telebusiness. It is the embodiment of so much that we aspire to—micro-segmentation down to the individual unit, fully interactive, measurable, data and information rich, controllable, and susceptible to very precise behavioural analysis.

Of course it has had a mixed press: invasive, insensitive, inappropriate and incompetently done, to name but four generic criticisms. But these relate to execution not concept. Similarly, the medium has been abused by get-rich-quick operators of dubious chatlines. These problems are likely to be with us for all time, but as the professional exploitation of the medium grows, they will diminish in importance. For the present they put a serious distortion upon the image of telebusiness.

In Chapter 12 we shall look at the impact of technology innovation upon marketing communications, but it is worth repeating here Wendy Aldiss's observation that telebusiness is migrating fast towards a state in which any communication via telephone media will be included in the term—whether digital data, voice or video content. Telebusiness will be seen as a branch of the multi-media industry—one that is forecast to grow at an exponential rate over the next 20 years. Thus, in thinking about the particular attributes of voice telephony within telebusiness, we should not lose sight of the fact that the key learning points will apply generically to multi-media as well. If you are a reluctant telebusiness user or aspirant today, ask yourself whether you are missing the opportunity to gain valuable experience now in a young technology, thereby establishing a competence level for the bigger things, just around the corner.

Earlier in the book I referred to the dilemma for direct marketers represented in the achievement of, say, a 5 per cent response from a mailing campaign. I stressed that another way of looking at the result is a 95 per cent non-response or failure. The worst thing that can happen to a forensic marketer is not knowing why something has, or has not, happened. It is surely an axiom of good marketing that if you can understand why a customer buys you can get them (and others) to do it again. That is the concept, but until telebusiness techniques became widely available, it has been difficult to put into practice cost effectively. Telebusiness has changed in so far as we are now able to ask buyers and non-buyers alike the whys and wherefores of their decision.

I rather doubt whether the market research techniques needed for this are yet refined enough to release the full potential of this approach, but the progress is encouraging. What is more restrictive is the psychological barrier to be overcome by many marketers wanting to explore why prospects did not buy: it means peering into the entrails of failure. I would argue that there is a full spectrum between the few customers who would have bought at any price and the few prospects who would never have bought at any price— different gradations of positivism or negativism. Bart Kosko (1994), in his insightful book *Fuzzy thinking*, reminds us that most things in life are not simple yes or no choices. Between yes and no are unlimited possibilities. These, familiar to the direct marketeer, constitute the clusters of significant variables found in regression analysis.

Where many marketers have been limited in their ability to improve performance is in the realm of moving from yes/no analysis to establishing the fuzzy continuum between those points. I believe that telebusiness offers, besides a potent tool for achieving direct sales, the best hope for detailed pre-facto, de facto and post-facto analysis of markets so that the continuum can, at the very least, be divided into meaningful clusters of positivism or negativism, opening the way for structured single variable tests of offers in pursuit of incremental effectiveness.

That might be seen as the ultimate rationale for the medium. On the way lie many benefits, enumerated by Wendy Aldiss, and too tempting I believe to ignore. Telebusiness, coupled with the cluster analysis techniques of geodemographics (see Chapter 10), allow for structured mass market testing. The knowledge gained has durable value and can be extrapolated to provide beneficial national profiles—the leverage of the two techniques is immense.

Even though I may seem only to be exhorting consumer-oriented marketers to seize the telephone, the principles apply in equal measure to the business-to-business marketer. It is true, regrettably, that reliable information on commercial clients, including their behaviour under various stimuli, is conspicuous by its absence. Generally there is too much reliance on transactional data, which may well mask the reasons why a buy decision was made. Forensic marketers understand customer and client behaviours. Telebusiness is the key to that competence.

## Questions to consider

**11.1**   What part in the marketing mix does telebusiness play now?
**11.2**   What else could telebusiness do to enhance the value of each element of the marketing mix?
**11.3**   What do we know about our customers?
**11.4**   What would we like to know?
**11.5**   What are the principal bands with the fuzzy decision continuum that we wish to define?
**11.6**   What do we know about non-buying prospects?
**11.7**   What would we like to know?
**11.8**   How large is the market that nearly bought?
**11.9**   How large is the market that nearly did not buy?
**11.10**  What systems have to capture both buyer and non-buyer information?
**11.11**  What competences do we need to make full use of telebusiness?
**11.12**  What uses of telebusiness can we make in serving other stakeholder communications?
**11.13**  What communications do we currently undertake that could be better canalized through telebusiness?

**11.14** What is the connection between effective relationship marketing and telebusiness?

**11.15** What is the competitive utilization of telebusiness and what is it likely to be over time?

**11.16** What use of tele-response mechanisms do we design into above-the-line advertising and what use ought we to make of them?

**11.17** What do we know about the likely technology developments in telebusiness, such as Integrated Services Digital Network (ISDN), interactive non-voice telephony, telephone-based payment systems and voice recognition developments?

**11.18** Where does telebusiness fit within our market research programme?

**11.19** Where ought it to be?

**11.20** What are the legal implications of telebusiness?

**11.21** What are the economics of telebusiness, both absolute cost and as cost of sale?

**11.22** What lessons can we learn from the growth in UK telebanking against the relative failure (to date) of TV and phone-based home-shopping systems?

**11.23** What is our ethical position on telebusiness to home- based consumers?

**11.24** How accessible are we as a business? Could telebusiness enhance our accessibility?

**11.25** What do we know about telebusiness support systems, from hardware and software vendors, including the telecomms industry?

Wendy Aldiss draws out a number of important points about the interpersonal skills that lie at the core of effective verbal telebusiness. The power of the technology is likely to be realized by those organizations that have a firm grip, if that is the word, on the softer skills of marketing. Telebusiness is a rare amalgam of highly measurable activities and often intuitive interpersonal skills. It is a young technology in relative terms and many marketers, particularly those who accept the rigour of the forensic approach, will want to make fast progress in the field. You cannot start telebusiness too soon.

# 12

# New technologies

## Anticipating their impact

### Monica E. Seeley (Mesmo Consultancy)

## Introduction by Gavin Barrett

Chapters 4–11 have in the main addressed the communications mix in terms of the here and now—reviewing techniques and arguments likely to be familiar to a significant proportion of readers. In this chapter I have asked Monica Seeley to review the emergent technologies that are likely to impact the roles and resources of marketers. Some of these technologies, like interactive multi-media, are already being used to good effect by marketers, for example in the leisure fields of music and travel, as well as automotive, financial services and real estate sectors.

Multi-media is a young technology, with much written about it, much claimed, and, as yet, only a little delivered. It is, however, likely to be one of the significant technologies available and relevant to almost all marketers.

Other technologies are still in the laboratory stage, pending the solution to major problems of mass application. Central to this group is the concept of image compression which will allow high-quality video digital data to be distributed at low cost and high speed through established telecomms networks, combined with interactive facilities. At the moment image compression is some way off that definition, albeit the compression ratios achieved in the laboratories of the major players already represent 90 per cent of the battle objectives.

Another factor that will undoubtedly change the face of marketing is the so-called concept of the Negroponte Switch, developed at the Massachusetts Institute of Technology (MIT), which demonstrates that whereas television has been a mainly broadcast technology, with modern enhancements through multinational satellite broadcasting systems, it is likely in future to be a mainly terrestrial technology, distributed to consumers via land-based systems of copper wire or fibre optics. Meanwhile telephony, which has been primarily a terrestrial system for the mass market, will become a broadcast technology, building on the formidable pioneering work in cellular networks.

The technology ins and outs of the Negroponte Switch need not concern us over much, although Monica Seeley provides more detail later in the chapter for readers who will see applications for their sector sooner rather than later. What the forensic marketer will need to think about are the implications of these twin phenomena.

The main implication will, I believe, lie in the precision with which marketers can reach markets, with unprecedented interactivity. Mass marketing has generally been a blunt instrument because of the technical limitations of the media available (television, radio and national media, for example). Now that will change: telephone numbers will become personal to the subscriber, rather than specific to a geographic location and will allow contact wherever and whenever desired. With the advent of digital telephone systems, these broadcast networks will support mobile fax, computing, and, when the image compression technology catches up, video transmission—and all with interactivity.

Similarly, with television becoming a terrestrially based technology, the ability to establish interactive links with the viewer become relatively straightforward. The cable TV operators are already well advanced in home shopping, home banking, security systems and information access facilities. As cable penetrates markets, or is supplemented with the same range of options via the telecomms networks, the influence on traditional views of television advertising, for example, will be massive. Of course, the debate rages in the advertising world that consumers will not want either the choices implicit in this new frontier technology or the interactive capability that goes with it. I find that too simplistic: some consumers will not change from passive viewers to active information and decision-taking correspondents, but a significant proportion will. Over time that proportion will grow to a point at which, with 30 per cent conversion to active behaviours, the economics become highly favourable. As with the penetration of PCs it has become a question of which generation are you talking about? The interactive scenario that I am painting is already familiar territory to millions of teenagers worldwide.

France has shown some of the potential with its Minitel information and transaction system, provided at low cost to any telephone subscriber who wants it and capable of providing vast amounts of data. Its limitations are mainly its unfriendliness to the user and the necessary precondition that subscribers know how to mine through data to find the information they want. None the less, it is a national system, effective, cheap and profitable. Minitel is a mass consumer decision-support system and is a powerful example of what will become commonplace: what will change for most of us will be the quality of service and ease-of-use of these systems.

Naturally, all these changes to established communications media bring threats as well as opportunities. Printed media are concerned about the current lack of interactivity to most of their advertising, but they are experimenting with telephone response support systems as I write. The advertiser now knows that within a short timespan it will be possible to target, with unitary precision, the homes and phones of highly segmented markets and obtain a response. On the other hand, tens of millions of people commuting to work each day will still, presumably, value their daily digest of news and features in a traditional newspaper. Or will they?

One scenario gaining ground is that consumers will specify what their interests are for news, current affairs, lifestyle and advertising and receive a highly tailored *newspaper-on-demand* via their domestic, office or mobile PC—allowing them to print out only the bits they want. These newspapers-on-demand will be continuously updated: one commmentator (Chronis, 1994) speaks of the 'hourly edition'. What is being transferred to the consumer is the power of editorial choice and, to some degree, the ability to side-step the blandishments of advertisers. Over time, publics will become more sophisticated in their ability to choose what they see, hear, read or do and it is this changing balance in the relationship between the *done-to* and the historic *doers* that marketers will need to come to terms with.

While much of this scenario painting has addressed mass consumer markets, the potential for new technologies to transform the way in which business-to-business marketing is conducted is equally dramatic. E-mail (electronic mail) and its derivatives are commonplace in linking organizations and their trading stakeholders together. Electronic data interchange (EDI) is well established in many industrial processes allowing the automatic placing of orders and payments between customers and suppliers—dramatically illustrated in the chemical sector where continuous process plant electronically senses the need for more material, places a direct order on the supplier's computer system, including all special requirements, and logs delivery allowing automatic payment transfer. No paperwork, no delay, and little room for error.

Integrated Services Digital Network (ISDN) has been around for some time, but is now beginning to be taken up. Its clever combination of simultaneous voice, video and digital transmission from one PC to another is transforming knowledge transfer and decision processes in many industries. As the users at either end (or station on a network) have identical information on their screens and any change made by one is immediately visible to the other, it becomes possible to draft contracts, literature, advertising copy and so on in real time, regardless of distance. Given that voice and video are part of the ISDN system, interpersonal communication is as well supported as the digital components.

Overarching all of the new technologies is the dramatic change in the way information is made available. It has become easier, by an order of magnitude, to become well informed about so much more than we used to. It is likely that we can take better decisions quicker as a result. We shall have more choice because we shall know more. Solutions offered to us will become more sophisticated because we shall be more sophisticated. Our expectations of information from suppliers will increase sharply. The amount of knowledge we shall be able to gain about our customers will, equally, increase on a massive scale. Just as it is commonplace for the food industry to have continuous real-time information from supermarket checkouts on what is bought and where, allowing extreme behavioural monitoring, so that will be normal in mass consumer transactions of every type.

This is a new world for marketers, whether a brave new world in the Aldous Huxley sense, or something more friendly, only time will tell. In the meantime, I am certain that forensic marketers will need to address these changes, become well informed about them and think through the consequences as they will apply to the marketing proposition between them and their customers, their use of the communications mix and, in the full sense of Hamel and Prahalad's (1991) expeditionary marketing, what new markets can be established, consolidated and exploited as a result, before the competition has woken up to the new reality.

Thus, while Monica Seeley's chapter is theoretically ahead of the context of this book, it seems to me to be wise to take a forward look. The rate of change is so fast and significant that many of the points we have described as coming may well have become established within a year or two. Others will never happen, and concepts we have not been able to imagine will be seen as obvious by the end of the nineties. The forensic marketer is unlikely to be complacent about his or her present reality.

## Introduction by Monica E. Seeley

As Gavin Barrett indicates, there is a growing range of new technologies which offer the forensic marketer an opportunity to gain a competitive edge, by either enhancing the response from a campaign or simply doing things better than the competition. While none of these new technologies directly replaces the media outlined in the earlier chapters each, as we shall see, can add considerable value to existing marketing activities as well as support the ability to be *well informed*. We shall undoubtedly see a shift in marketing spend from traditional forms of advertising towards more emphasis on the use of the newer cable and interactive television media. Indeed these technologies will lead to a complete rethink about the criteria for determining when to advertise, because there will no longer be peak viewing times. Other factors such as duration of advertisements and response mechanisms to them will need rethinking.

From the bagatelle of new technology, here are the ten which at the time of writing look the most promising and the most likely to influence the basis upon which marketing is undertaken:

- Image compression and fibre optics
- Multi-media
- Integrated Services Digital Network (ISDN)
- Cable and interactive television
- Mobile telephony
- Groupware
- Internet
- Personal digital assistants (PDAs)
- Virtual reality (VR)
- Neural networks.

These technologies create an *information paradox* for the marketer. On the one hand, technologies such as Internet and PDAs enable us to generate a torrent of information, in the face of which some may feel overwhelmed. On the other hand, technologies such as groupware and neural networks provide us with the tools to process, analyse, and share huge volumes of information at speeds and with accuracy which were undreamt of, until the mid-nineties.

Broadly speaking there are five ways in which the emerging technologies can help us as marketeers. They are outlined below and summarized in Table 12.1:

- Communicating our message more effectively and efficiently
- Improving the quality of information available and our ability to share it with others involved in the decision-making process
- Bringing new services and products to market more quickly
- Changing the basis upon which we do business
- Improving our personal effectiveness as marketers.

**Table 12.1** Potential impact of different technologies on the marketing process

|  | Communicating the message effectively | Improved information processing | Bringing new services and products to market faster | Changing the basis for business | Improving personal productivity |
|---|---|---|---|---|---|
| Image compression | ✓ |  | ✓ | ✓ |  |
| Multi-media | ✓ |  | ✓ |  | ✓ |
| ISDN | ✓ | ✓ | ✓ | ✓ | ✓ |
| Cable and interactive TV | ✓ | ✓ | ✓ | ✓ |  |
| Mobile telephony | ✓ | ✓ | ✓ | ✓ | ✓ |
| Groupware |  | ✓ |  |  | ✓ |
| Internet | ✓ | ✓ |  | ✓ | ✓ |
| PDAs | ✓ | ✓ |  |  | ✓ |
| Virtual reality |  | ✓ | ✓ |  |  |
| Neural networks |  | ✓ | ✓ |  |  |

## Image compression and fibre optics

Underlying many of the new forms of technology and especially interactive television and multi-media and the information highway are developments in the fields of image compression and fibre optics (*Business Week*, 13 June 1994). Image compression enables information (in any format, audio, text and image) to be converted from traditional analogue format into digital format which can then be compressed for transmission and storage in a fraction of the space previously required. Developments in fibre optics mean that vastly increased band-widths are available to transmit information. For example ten television channels can now be transmitted across a band-width which in the late eighties could transmit only one.

Neither technology is new: both have been around for decades. What is new is the meeting of the minds of technology and media giants such as AT&T and Time-Warner to exploit the combination of the two technologies to create brave new worlds which enable us to create interactive communications in ways and speeds hitherto unknown. It will be possible to transmit a multi-media presentation faster than the fastest fax and, of course, in colour. The developments in image compression and fibre optics underpin the developments in cable and interactive television, ISDN and multi-media.

## Multi-media

Multi-media is the word used to describe a computer-based presentation which incorporates text, graphics, digital sound, computer output, and video all on one storage medium. To date the main uses for multi-media have been within training, as a method of delivering highly interactive distance learning materials, point-of-sale activities, and within the leisure industry for home entertainment (Latchem *et al.*, 1993). However, there are five areas (*Business Week*, 12 July 1993) within marketing where multi-media will be used to enhance the communications process and provide business benefits:

- Development of presentations
- Design of promotional materials
- Development of corporate image
- Strengthening customer loyalty
- Video conferencing.

Before we look at each use, let us consider what is known about how we absorb and remember information. For most people information retention increases directly with the number of different information processing channels being utilized, and the level of interactivity. That is to say we are more likely to remember and understand a message if we can engage and use both our audio and visual channels of processing rather then just visual. Similarly we shall remember more if we interact with the presentation, for example by answering questions rather than sitting passively.

Multi-media technology provides the opportunity to capitalize on both these well-proven theories of human information processing, and hence communicate our message far more effectively and efficiently than if we rely on one, and at best two media, such as traditional video.

## Development of presentations

The time we have to create a favourable impression and gain customers' or prospects' attention is very short. Think back over the last few times when you have been on the receiving end of a marketing or sales presentation. How quickly did you start to form an impression of whether or not you wanted to deal with that person or organization? On what did you base your judgement? I can assert that a key factor was the quality of the visual aids. Multi-media can help provide sales and marketing presentations which

- Are of the highest quality and make an immediate impact
- Utilize a wide variety of communications channels and hence optimize the chances of prospects and customers remembering your message
- Can be made interactive and not passive, so again improve the chances of the message being remembered
- Bring life to the presentation and convey a high level of reality
- Provide structural continuity within the presentation while incorporating a range of media sources.

A handful of organizations are already using multi-media techniques to good effect and finding benefits such as a significant decrease in the sales time needed to sell complex products. I suggest that multi-media based presentations will become the norm over the next few years to a point at which any salesperson and marketer who does not use this technology is certain to be at a disadvantage. Moreover, the interactive nature of multi-media provides an as yet untapped source of data about your clients and prospects.

## Design of promotional materials

Desk-top publishing revolutionized the production of paper-based monochrome promotional materials. However, the production of colour materials, especially those with plenty of graphics, is still primarily the domain of the specialist design house. Multi-media offers the potential for significantly improving what can still be a costly and time-consuming task. Multi-media helps the planning and design of the creative approach and the final artwork. How many times do we make last-minute changes to the creative elements or the artwork? The cost goes up and so does the production time. Multi-media eliminates some of the problems because we can see the end product immediately. If those needing to approve the artwork are geographically dispersed then consider an ISDN link (see below), instead of the conventional courier, for distributing the materials.

## Development of corporate image

There are a number of areas surrounding the development and communication of the corporate image where multi-media offers significant advantages. Take a situation wherein your product offerings are complex and promotion of them would benefit from the client seeing a realistic simulation of what the future will be like after the acquisition of the product. Typical examples would be a motor car, a new piece of technology, or a drug. Multi-media can help provide just such a simulation presentation, conveying a realistic image of the product and, thereby, shorten the sales cycle.

If you are running a television media campaign, consider the impact on the client of a sales presentation which reinforces the television campaign by incorporating the same visual material. This is largely only possible with multi-media, which can incorporate video images.

## Strengthening client loyalty

The more ways in which it is made easy for customers to buy, the more likely they are to stay. Conversely you are seeking to make it more difficult for them to switch out of the relationship. A powerful way to do this is to put buying aids *on the customer's* desk. Examples include your catalogue, a link to your order entry systems—via electronic data interchange (EDI)—estimating and forecasting tools. For example, this might mean the components your client needs either to manufacture products or to provide other services. But before customers can order from you they must work out quantities and precise specifications. Relationship marketers provide clients with the tools to make their life easier.

Increasingly corporations from financial services to component manufacturers are already exploiting multi-media within the marketing context in the ways outlined here and gaining distinct business and competitive benefits.

## Video conferencing

Until the advent of multi-media and ISDN, video conferencing had been the prerogative of the very largest organizations and took place only in a specially equipped studio. However, it is becoming possible to run a desk-based video conference using the technologies of multi-media and ISDN at quite low costs. Such ideas have already found a home in the thinking of leading players in the financial services sector in the USA and UK. Boeing found that it could cut back some project times by 90 per cent by using video conferencing linked to groupware. While the automated teller machine (ATM) can be used to provide more and more services, there will always be a need for some human interface to deal with questions and provide personal and expert advice. This can be done by video conferencing, even though the customer and the banker are separated geographically. Think too of the potential for running focus research groups. Video conferencing looks set to take off again and this time be accessible to all.

## Integrated Services Digital Network (ISDN)

Integrated Services Digital Network is the telecommunications technology which allows the transmission of text, audio and images between personal computers. The main distinction between this and video conferencing is that with ISDN at its present stage of development one cannot simultaneously see the person with whom one is communicating. However, if that is not a mandatory prerequisite, then ISDN offers some exciting potential. To do both requires a combination of ISDN and video conferencing using technology like BT's PC videophone.

## Cable and interactive television

Much has already been written about these increasingly familiar forms of television. With interactive TV consumers can provide specific information about their needs; in response, material is transmitted to meet these needs, including advertisements, information, or programmes. Users include the Ford Motor Company and General Motors in the USA. Conversely the buyer (consumer and business) can browse though catalogues and order directly, interacting only with the television set. Such technology is being used extensively in the USA and in limited ways in the UK, especially in clothing and consumer electronics.

There is no doubt that cable and interactive TV will take off. The breakthrough is likely when digital TV becomes the norm, which is some time ahead. Meanwhile, there is plenty to be gained from exploring the potential of these media and being ready to exploit.

## Mobile telephony

Phone numbers will become personal numbers, and remain so for life. Thus, if consumers can escape from the conventional television advertisement there may be scope to recapture them through the telephone. Moreover, there can never be any excuse for us, as marketers, being out of reach.

## Groupware

How often have you tried to prepare a marketing brief and involve all who need to be involved, only to find them either reading from different versions of the copy, or unavailable to read the copy and provide a timely input. Groupware is software which allows organizations to share information on a PC network, regardless of location and time. However, unlike ISDN, only text and images are shared on the screen. But the information that is shared is the same for everyone and, as updates are made, so they are shared with everyone immediately.

Currently groupware is being exploited for creating shared database for sales account management, customer service, document management, and new product development in which many people need access to the same information, at every stage. The principal benefits come from reduced error rates and lower usage of time and thus cost. Organizations finding these benefits include Reebok, Texaco, British Airways, Price Waterhouse and Lotus, the latter being the leading supplier of groupware software (called Notes).

## Internet

The Internet (or network of networks, as it is sometimes known) is a global network which allows you to access, communicate and share information regardless of time and location. Unlike ISDN or interactive and cable television, the Internet is a text-based only system. However, it is relatively inexpensive and thus accessible by

organizations and consumers. As a result many are already on-line.
Upwards of 20 million are estimated to be on Internet. Current uses
include gathering and analysing competitor intelligence, creating
*bulletin boards* about your products and services, providing public
reports, recruitment searches, and patent searches, and decision
support. The Internet is a little like an on-line encyclopedia. If you
need information you will undoubtedly find it on the Internet.
Conversely it offers one of the fastest ways of communicating
messages to other users on Internet. Through Internet you can
log in to your own organization's e-mail from anywhere in the
world.

## Personal digital assistants (PDAs)

A PDA is a hand-held computer with the capacity of a very
powerful workstation. A PDA allows you to enter data using
conventional handwriting or freehand drawings. In the case of the
latter it will then automatically tidy up your sketch and leave you
with a near-perfect graphic on the screen. A PDA has diary
management, contact and database management, fax facilities, and
common software applications such as word processing and
spreadsheets. Data can be exchanged between the PDA and main
computer systems. Leading players in this market include AT&T
and Apple computers with their Newton.

PDAs and, in particular, the Newton offer the potential to

- Overcome the socially unacceptable side of the laptop, especially
  within the sales situation
- Convert the esoteric into reality
- Cut down on the paperwork involved in agreeing or confirming a
  sale
- Improve communications externally
- Improve the flow of information around the organization
- Capture broader-based information about your customers.

## Virtual reality (VR)

Virtual reality (VR) is a computer-based system which allows one to
model the real world on a PC, while providing visual, audio, and
tactile reality in response to body movements. Such body
movements are detected and analysed electronically. To date, the
major uses of VR have been as highly sophisticated high-reality

simulations for training (Rheingold, 1991) and the larger market of arcade games.

However, there does seem to be some potential in it for the marketing function in terms of market research on new products, which may as yet be little more than an idea on the drawing board. Virtual reality affords the opportunity to test new products and ideas before incurring major production costs such as shop layouts. Indeed the textile industry is starting to exploit the technology via the creation of a *virtual catwalk* on which new designs for garments can be market tested before a cut is made in the cloth. Link this to video conferencing, and focus group research starts to take on a new dimension.

## Neural networks

Neural computing, and hence networks, originate from the world of artificial intelligence. Neural networks simulate the way our biological brains work. They can deal with fuzzy and incomplete data to produce a model or approximation (Beale and Jackson, 1994). They gain their intelligence from being 'trained' on real data, usually historic in the first place. However, a neural network is the epitome of the well-informed individual as it goes on learning, updating the basis upon which it makes decisions and as it receives new data.

Some companies (including Thomas Cook and several financial service organizations) are starting to use neural networks to help them plan and analyse their direct marketing. Neural computing can take an incomplete database and provide buyer profiles, many of which are beyond the profiling systems based on current conventional statistical methods, such as regression and cluster analysis.

One of the major problems facing any airline is how accurately to predict seat occupancy and the level of overbooking. Neural networks are providing some of the answers. The Airline Marketing Tactician has been found to predict resource allocation far more efficiently and effectively.

Within the financial services sector a neural network-based system to assess loan and default rating was found to be more accurate than the human decision-making process so that a 7 per cent increase in profits could be achieved. The use of neural networks is already quite extensive within the financial sector.

# The limiting factors

As every marketer knows, there is no such thing as a free lunch, and none of the above technologies is without its drawbacks. First, there are the hardware and software issues. For all these technologies to truly revolutionize the way we do business, whether on a business-to-consumer or business-to-business market-place they must be operable and accessible from the desk-top PC, whether that means that the desk-top is fixed or mobile, or a home TV, whatever shape that will take in future. These technologies all need significant levels of processing power and special circuit boards and CD-ROMs. Such PCs are still not readily found on most desks or in most homes. This will become less of a problem as more powerful PCs become available at cheaper prices; but when the optimized cross-over will happen between cost and power for mass market penetration is another matter.

Second, there is the competition within the technology industry itself, with each manufacturer striving to establish its system as the de facto standard. This is particularly marked around the multi-media and interactive TV technologies as the big players fight to provide the dominant viewing device, the PC or the television screen.

Third, there is the gap between the capability of the technology and our own competence to use it. This gap will undoubtedly be eroded in time as more acquire the necessary technical skills and knowledge to use these technologies to their full potential.

Fourth, and perhaps more fundamentally, there is a generally negative attitude among managers to be innovative. Innovation means taking risks and being able to think and solve problems inductively. There are skills and attributes that many lack. We are far too steeped in the traditional deductive approaches to problem-solving whereby we either wait for a problem to arise and then seek out the technology, or we wait for someone else to burn their fingers. Have no doubt that the innovators will gain the high ground in terms of information management and all the advantages that will bring. (Davenport, 1993, and Hammer and Champy, 1993.)

Fifth, there are the socially acceptable standards. For some (clients and suppliers) technology is a total anathema, while others may shun you and your organization if you are not using technology to communicate and provide services (Mitroff and Linstone, 1993). You will undoubtedly need to test-market your use of technology and may even need to do some old-fashioned segmentation, as to who and how you make your offer using new technology.

Sixth, there is cost. None of these technologies is currently cheap and, adding in the cost of change necessary for success, you are looking at a significant investment. While the underlying base costs of PCs and telecommunications are falling, you will need to weigh up the price that you are prepared to pay for relative competitive leadership against the lower cost of being a follower.

Last, but by no means least, is obsolescence. Technology is changing so fast that what is state of the art now may be old hat tomorrow. Obsolescence means new ways of accounting for and valuing the technology investment. What is also important is to maintain a *balanced* technology portfolio of the tried and tested and the innovative.

## Keeping well informed about technological developments

Do not wait to read about such developments in the marketing press. By then the information will be second-hand, based on a deductive opinion, and be stripped of its real significance. Attend the trade show and read for yourself the computer press (such as *Computing, Computer Weekly,* etc.). Talk to the professional technologist in your IT department. Above all, make your own first-hand well-informed judgement about the value and potential of these (and other) technological developments to you and your organization.

## Checklist

It is easy to forget just how much development in technology there has been in the few years since Sir Clive Sinclair launched his first LED (light-emitting diode) calculator at £100 in the early eighties. That same calculator specification, now housed in a credit card format, costs less than £0.50. It is forecast that within a decade the processing power of the PC will have increased by a factor of 40 at a cost which will have declined in real terms by a factor of 10 (Printing Industry Research Association 1991). Indeed, the rate of innovation is such that the marketer must find ways and means of understanding the underlying technologies rather than specific products, as these latter will have very transient lives. The race by the likes of Xerox Corporation, IBM, Microsoft, Apple, AT&T, Time-Warner, and Cable and Wireless, as well as telecomms operators worldwide, to master the technologies of image compression so that high-resolution video images can be transmitted via telecomms networks on demand is likely to be resolved well before the millennium. The pilot initiatives in the USA by Time-Warner allow some 500 *channels* to be distributed in parallel throughout large parts of Florida, giving the consumer unimaginable choice. This formidable capability, coupled with interactive systems, will perhaps revolutionize not only the entertainment industry, but also personal financial management, home security and information retrieval, let alone home shopping.

The challenge for the marketer is not only to understand the basis of the technologies but also to develop the imagination to harness them within the marketing mix. It has been asserted by leading media owners that it will be the ability to supply information on demand and in customer specific formats that will differentiate the high performance companies of the next 20 years, rather than cost revenue productivity management. Imagination will be the most valued competence. Monica Seeley, in her tour d'horizon, has concentrated on the immediately available technologies and, in particular, multi-media. Already well established in high-ticket retail merchandising, especially the motor industry, its applications are increasingly visible in business-to-business marketing. Special applications in the fields of education, travel and management information have changed the outlook of whole sectors.

## Questions to consider

**12.1**  What are the technologies currently available for our business area?

**12.2**  How well do we understand these existing technologies?

**12.3**  What new technologies are anticipated which have application to our business?

**12.4**  What mechanisms have we for monitoring technology innovation?

**12.5**  What mechanisms have we for evaluating technology innovations?

**12.6**  What use are we making of information systems to enhance our marketing decisions?

**12.7**  What account of technology change have we taken in developing our marketing strategy?

**12.8** Which technologies would enhance our data-gathering effectiveness?

**12.9** How well integrated are our data sources, allowing us to take well-informed decisions?

**12.10** What technology-based communications would enhance our relationships with business-to-business customers, or intermediate stages in the distribution chain?

**12.11** What are the creative skills needed to ensure that new technologies do not become mere gimmicks in our marketing mix?

**12.12** What impact will cable-based systems have on consumer viewing and buying behaviours?

**12.13** What impact will cable-based systems have on the advertising industry?

**12.14** What impact do we expect technology to have on general levels of literacy?

**12.15** What impact do we expect technology to have on time to market for new product development?

**12.16** What scope do the new technologies offer for increasing personal customization of products and services in our sector?

**12.17** Which technologies do we expect to see having a major impact on retail selling?

**12.18** Which technologies will have a major impact on face-to-face selling?

**12.19** What are the potential uses of automatic teller machines?

**12.20** Should we lead or follow in the introduction of technology-based marketing?

**12.21** What are the critical success factors for achieving the optimum benefits from technology innovation in our business?

**12.22** What are our priorities for technology overall?

**12.23** Where are we going to acquire the new skills to optimize the potential of new technologies?

**12.24** Who are the bench-mark organizations for technology application that we could network with?

**12.25** How well informed do we need to be to survive and prosper?

Rather a challenging set of questions perhaps, but illustrative of the dilemma facing marketing professionals. There have been too many expensively embraced innovations in recent years for marketers not to remember the pain and the scars—the long trench-war between the VHS, Betamax and VCC formats in video, for example—and to have developed some degree of technophobia. However, ostrich-like behaviour is highly risky given the sledge-hammer blows that some technologies will deliver to mature, seemingly well-founded businesses, such as newspapers, banking, education, legal services, telecomms and inter-company trading in general.

We shall all, no doubt, back some losers, but I believe that if we concentrate on the access to, added value to and distribution of information as the critical focus, we shall not be far wrong. To do nothing about new technologies is not an option.

# 13

# Common ground, valuable differences

## Making sense of the choices

Chapters 4 to 12 graphically illustrate the marketer's dilemma—too many choices, too little budget. In reality, however, most marketers make a judgement about the two or three techniques within the communications mix that they intend to use, conducting their 'beauty parades' accordingly. The choice is between suppliers of the marketer's predetermined solutions rather than an evaluation of which techniques best could meet the need and in what combination. Believing this to be a less than ideal approach I have sought to challenge it by providing a wider-than-usual range of choices, articulated by powerful professional advocates, so that readers may see the potential in general and of new and original combinations of communications techniques in particular. It is certainly a wider choice than many of us draw upon. It can also be wider still: I have not included the role of the salesforce nor the full panoply of sales promotion techniques, for example. The nine options provided in these chapters do, however, represent the lion's share of bought-in expenditure for most marketers.

At the end of each chapter I have proposed a short checklist questionnaire which will help determine the appropriateness, or otherwise, of each individual technique in meeting the particular marketing need. Since marketers ought to be rigorous about finding the problem before the solution, I am hopeful that readers will empathize with the challenge implicit in the checklists: 'Am I making the right use of this or that approach?' The enemy is, of course, precedent—if it worked before then it will work again. Fair enough at one level—risk avoidance—since trying out new ways of meeting the objective is always risky. Not to try out new ways is riskier still. Less easy to justify is the unvarying use of fixed combinations of communications tools, based on precedent, wherein the added value of each is not known, nor the particular attributes that work well in combination, but not necessarily so in isolation.

Consider the communications options in a government privatization programme. First, the target audiences are complex and diverse, ranging from political lobbies who need to be persuaded, to investment institutions, individual investors, existing customers, existing suppliers, existing staff, future potential customers, competitors, future employees, regulatory authorities and individual local communities. I could go further and break each of these segments into more precisely defined groupings, each with their own agenda. I certainly need to be able to define them with some precision if they are to be addressed on their own specific agenda, rather than some turkey-shoot catch-all platform.

Second, the three generic questions: 'What do we want them to know?' 'What do we want them to feel?' and 'What do we want them to do?' In each case very different answers will be found.

Third, what tools are available? Direct mail, public relations, above-the-line advertising, telemarketing, briefings or seminars and exhibitions come easily to mind. But which is right for which segment? Readers will have widely differing views, as will their professional suppliers. Yet I am fairly sure that consensus would emerge that above-the-line would be important, public relations (in the fullest sense) equally so, and direct marketing tools where specific individual actions are required—sending for the issue prospectus, for example.

Fourth, while the success of the privatization is the goal of government, it is merely the beginning for many other stakeholders, facing different futures and elements of real uncertainty. What should the communications strategy be to create the conditions for durable success beyond the first milestone of privatization? Here the question of corporate image looms large—it is the focus of the strategic positioning of the enterprise both prior to, and beyond, the historical moment of change. Furthermore, the question arises as to how far the new management will want their hands tied by pre-privatization image building, let alone explicit commitments made. How can they possibly know before they take charge?

We could go on exploring the ever-widening circles of dilemma facing our hypothetical privatization enterprise, but it must be obvious, even within this brief exploration, that the deployment of the full range of communications tools is more a question of an integrated plan than of the valuation of the individual merits of each one. No one communications task can be divorced from another— because the cross-over effect may be unknown. This is a statement of the obvious as far as the run-up to our privatization is concerned. It is less obviously so for life after 'P-day'. A maxim for all those engaged in this sort of activity might well look like this: 'Be sure you know where you want to end up before you start the journey'.

Translating this challenge to the more straightforward everyday communications tasks faced by marketers in commerce and industry, the lesson is clear. Each objective is only a milestone. Consequently, marketers have, I believe, to face the real discomfort of the discipline of playing the long game. Every marketing action has a past and a future.

This is what gives this book its particular orientation in helping the marketer view the task of marketing communications in as objective a light as possible, because to do the other, succumbing too easily to the individual blandishments of one technique versus another is to miss the point entirely. It is the guardianship of an integrated and continuous communications strategy that must precondition almost all tactical decisions.

The aphorism that there are no second chances at first impressions is cautionary enough for those contemplating a new market. It is as nothing in terror terms when compared with the notion that once you have started you must continue. By this I mean that every communication to a segment (right down to the individual level) is inevitably linked to what preceded it and what succeeds it. At least that ought to be the case. Those members of the UK clearing bank community basking in the full glow of dynamic market growth in the late eighties paid, it would seem, scant regard to their future potential in pursuing a relentless product-driven scatter-gun communications strategy, often ill-segmented and always super-tactical. The British Chancellor of the Exchequer, in his 1990 Budget Statement, rightly admonished the sector for the 'indiscriminate promotion of credit, especially to those who could ill-afford to take it'. He might well have gone on to chastise the same people for having destroyed, in a few ill-conceived tactical campaigns, their brand values built up over centuries, betokening financial rectitude and good sense.

Like it or not, there is a continuum to marketing communications which should be recognized and respected. In evaluating the choices available to the marketer, as represented in Chapters 4 to 12, it is important, I believe, to be able to test each for its fit within this continuum—does each lend itself to the long game as well as the short? Since this continuum is often expressed in terms of core brand values, it might be as well to think of it thus.

I argue the point about the continuity of marketing communications because it seems clear that markets, in the reality of the purchase decision, value confidence in the product or service (and its supplier) higher than choice. If the reverse were true then we could all live happily ever after in a tactical free-for-all. But it is not—most of us are concerned with gaining and retaining markets, securing growth however we can and believing that trysting in a warm bed is much to be preferred to cold encounters of any kind. We cannot, therefore, put tactics first.

Assuming that you accept the premise that the goal comes before the getting, it is useful to have a checklist of questions that fix the backdrop against which the play will be made.

## Journey's end checklist

**13.1**  What are our core brand values?

**13.2**  How do we know they are?

**13.3**  What should our core brand values be, and in whose opinion?

**13.4**  How much flexibility do we want from our brand values?

**13.5**  How much clarity does our statement of purpose (mission) provide for defining our communications strategy?

**13.6**  How clear are the milestones in brand development that will guide us towards our internal vision?

**13.7**  How well have we defined our core stakeholders (e.g. investors, customers, suppliers, employees, bankers)?

**13.8**  How well have we defined our relationship strategy with each?

**13.9**  How clearly have we resolved the strategic tension between adding to shareholder value and customer service quality? Do we see any tension?

**13.10** How necessary is it for us to have sustainable relationships with the stakeholders?

**13.11** What is the long-term basis of our competitive advantage— from differentiation to cost?

**13.12** What ought to be the long-term basis of our competitive advantage, what are our core competences that we must be valued for by our stakeholders?

**13.13** What have we learned from monitoring our competitors' long-term behaviours in communication terms?

**13.14** What have we learned from analysing our own past communications behaviours?

**13.15** How well does our business planning process take account of the need to develop and implement a consistent communications strategy?

**13.16** How precisely have we defined our values and beliefs that will inform our communications plan? The things we will always say and those that we will never say?

**13.17** How much do we know about the barriers to sustainable relationships with our stakeholders?

**13.18** How willing are we to accept the discipline of a communications strategy?

**13.19** How do we avoid the perils of a five-year plan, with rigor mortis already set in, without living the high-risk life of just-in-time strategy formulation?

**13.20** What proportion of our revenue are we prepared to budget for strategic relationship development with our core stakeholders?

This checklist may look obvious, but just pause and ask yourself the question 'If I can answer all these questions, will my colleagues also come to the same conclusions?' After all, a communications strategy is no more and no less than an expression of the tenets that bind an organization together. If it is not the 'will of you all' will it be deliverable?

I have emphasized the need to develop this backdrop since, without it, the use of communications techniques from the kaleidoscope available will perhaps too easily represent the end rather than the means. In Chapter 1, I referred to the natural and important factor of ego-driven marketing—the feel and flair for great marketing ideas. I would not suppress that drive for a moment. All I do plead is that the ego-powered energy of marketers is canalized through a strategic process, rather than tactical enthusiasms.

Sadly, it is immensely difficult to maintain a strategically consistent course. I have already mentioned the trap of the 'fourth quarter fire fight' when strategy is tipped overboard just as readily as the women and children. Even so it must be striven for.

A major breakthrough will be achieved when the suppliers of professional marketing services either offer an integrated portfolio of techniques that serves the strategic communications agenda or are willing to work in open collaboration with their fellow suppliers in agreeing the givens by which all will abide. The former is, increasingly, on offer—whether it is a reality is another question, but as with all heterodox organizations, getting any sort of cross-party consistency (let alone conformity) is a tall order. We, as clients, should be very demanding in this respect, if only to help the one-stoppers achieve deliverable internal alignment as the basic condition of contract. The latter solution is very much down to the client to make it possible for diverse suppliers to work together. Whether this means a primus inter pares or, more simply, a joint briefing process is a matter for individual circumstance. One of the purposes of this book is to help suppliers in one field of the communications mix to see what their counterparts elsewhere think and say—I hope that they will understand better the origins of so many needless turf issues.

Clients cause turf issues by tolerating them on the one hand and being ambiguous on the other. Lack of clarity in the briefing process when dealing with any professional supplier is serious when just one supplier is involved. It is a capital crime when dealing with a pack of them. It is this question of integrating supplier talents that next colours our evaluation process of each of the siren calls made in Chapters 4 to 12. How do they fit together to achieve a seamless join?

## The supplier jigsaw

Jigsaw puzzles do not, of course, start life in pieces. No more should the communications plan. I stress should.

The overall picture must be visualized clearly since it is something we are going to have to look at and like for a long time to come. Then it can be divided up into interesting pieces—interesting to the supplier and the client. Implementation of the communications plan is the putting together of the jigsaw itself.

Each of us, no doubt, has a preferred approach to jigsaws. I tend to find the four corner pieces, followed by the edge pieces—that at least dimensions the task. The same applies to the communications plan—what are the corner pieces? How do we dimension the whole?

I have argued that the 20 point checklist earlier in the chapter will provide the main architectural framework, defining many of the outer pieces of our jigsaw. Other pieces in the puzzle come from having a number of tactical tasks—product launches, call cycles or follow-through campaigns, annual reports, half-time and full-year results, life-cycle modifications and the like. But because this is a jigsaw, each of these tactical pieces must fit with the others around them.

The same metaphor applies to the suppliers, who are also pieces in our jigsaw. Which fits with which? Extending the image a little way, we might allocate above-the-line and PR to the sky pieces, whereas relationship marketing and geodemographics belong to the detailed foreground. Given the cases put forward in Chapters 4 to 12 you can judge where they each see the natural links between them.

It goes without saying that it is far easier to complete the puzzle if a copy of the final picture is always to hand. Only when the picture is complete must we drop this metaphor, because it is at the very moment of triumphant completion that the puzzler may succumb to the temptation to break it all up and start again. If the picture is worth completing it is worth keeping.

There are no rules, I believe, for saying that one technique must always be used in this or that combination with others. What is at issue is which technique is best for which stage in the continuum? It is clear that corporate image is always the key to providing the backdrop: without a well-developed sense of image throughout all functional areas of the organization there can be no consistency of communication to all stakeholders. Yet it is a constant surprise that either it is not addressed at all or it is changed at will. Corporate image, as Wally Olins has stated, is the core set of perspectives from which corporate opportunities are viewed. It would be difficult to argue that corporate image comes anywhere but everywhere in the continuum.

That said, the rest of the communications tool-set is less obviously positioned. It depends very much on what the continuum actually is. So before moving on let us consider in a little more detail what I mean by the communications continuum.

## The communications continuum

Unless your organization is brand new, it has a past and, since you have joined it, hopefully a future. It has relationships with its stakeholders in varying degrees of maturity. It has goals and a sense of purpose—the latter which it probably wants to communicate to all stakeholders. It has past customers, now lapsed, present customers and it has potential customers yet to be found or won. It has past products or services, current offerings and a belief that it can create more in future. It has retired staff, current employees and children that are yet unborn as potential employees.

In the midst of these continua are the old favourites of product life cycle, Boston Consulting Group's (1971) *Stars, Queries, Cash Cows and Dogs*, Hamel and Prahalad's (1991) *Core Competences model*, Porter's (1985) *Value-Chain* and new models of lifestage and lifetime value definition.

It is on to and off these continuous escalators that we marketers must step adroitly with our interventions. Not in the Shakespearian sense of strutting and fretting our hour upon the stage and then being heard no more, but conscious of the need to add value to each moment as well as the momentum of corporate growth and success.

The question in determining how to make use of the powerful tools available for communications is more to do with 'Where will it lead?' than with 'What will it do now?' The latter, however, is where we too often get stuck, since it is what we, as marketers, are paid to deliver.

Another way of putting 'Where will it lead?' is 'What will it leave behind?' I have already touched upon the notion of organizations viewing marketing as the resource which pushes out the frontiers of experience so that it becomes wiser through experience. In the Forensic mnemonic *I* stands for *inertia* (see Chapter 3) and betokens the constant challenge to marketers to understand why things happen or why they do not. It is critical that organizations value discovery of better ways of doing things. For this purpose the scientific principles I have advanced for the Forensic approach become vital. Similarly, only some of the communications tools lend themselves readily to scientific analysis. I stress readily because it is possible to determine measurable impacts of all aspects of the communications mix if you set out to do so. Whether it is worth doing so is a matter for judgement.

However, there can be no progress without learning from experience and if there is one macro lesson from considering the continuum approach to marketing communications it is the responsibility of marketers to try and test new approaches to old problems from which learning can be achieved. It is not the task of marketers to reinvent the wheel. It is, however, a major duty for all marketing-minded people to recognize that there is always a better way and hence the supreme value in using communications suppliers to challenge both the status quo and the lessons of history: the professional marketer simply ensures that this does not mean reinventing the wheel.

Finally, I subscribe to the view that it is through close interaction with professional suppliers in marketing communications that we stand the best chance of finding the hidden markets—the people who nearly buy—the markets that nearly happened. This is surely the last frontier for marketers—tapping the key to why the sale did not happen.

We have thus considered the mind of the marketer in evaluating what our siren chorus has had to say. We think long and we think hard and we think consequences. But is that it?

The answer is not quite: there is the small matter, as I mentioned in the opening chapters of the book, of selling your enlightened view of the communications task to your boss. This will be the burden of the final chapter.

# 14

# Back to the start-line?

## Selling it to your boss

Thus far we have explored the relationship between top management's business strategy agenda, the role of marketing professionals in interacting with the client environment, thereby developing a relevant marketing strategy and the harnessing of powerful external resources in a coherent fashion, supported by the FORENSIC technique, to achieve outstanding implementation of both the high-level business and marketing strategies (see Fig. 14.1, which is Fig. 1.2 repeated here for easy reference).

In Chapter 13 I argued that it is the strategic view of the stakeholder relationship continua that must inform the marketer's actions, rather than solely concentrating upon tactical campaigning aimed at near-term objectives. That, at any rate, is the logical model. I am confident that you are nodding in agreement at this point. But how realistic is this concept? The answer, like so many in business, is a function of what is meant by realistic. I mean 'Can it be achieved?' At one level of rationality it is entirely possible to set a strategic framework for marketing communications and work within it.

Business life, however, is seldom rational and we shall need to take account of political realities in securing corporate-wide agreement to the serious discipline of working within a strategic framework. In every business there are a host of myths and legends which form the political milieu: finance functions are infallible: salespeople see the world through rose-tinted spectacles; operations do not care about customers; marketing is one big 'jolly'; general management is out of touch; customers are a nuisance and disrupt the smooth running of the organization. You could go on and on and get more and more depressed. Yet against this stereotypic backdrop of prejudice and assumption, the forensic marketer must seek to make

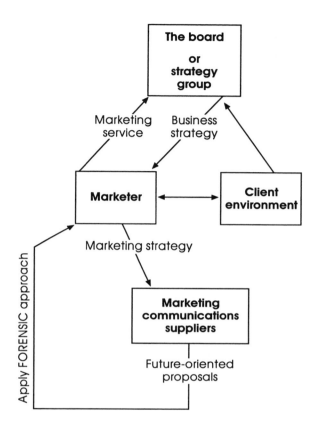

**Figure 14.1** Applying the FORENSIC model to the decision-making processes of the marketing function

progress and deliver sustainable competitive advantage. In this final chapter we shall examine what can be done to install the better way.

The start-line is the business strategy. I have always felt that organizations would do better to adopt a retrospective approach to strategy formulation rather than a prospective one. By this I mean working backwards from, say, a 10 years into the future milestone, towards a 5 year view and then a 1 year view, whereas the commonplace is to adopt a 1-5-10 approach (see Fig. 14.2).

I see a 10-5-1 method (and it could easily be 12-5-2 or a similar range) as providing a completely different perspective from the 1-5-10. First, we are exhorted by Hamel and Prahalad (1991), in their exemplary *Harvard Business Review* article, 'Corporate imagination

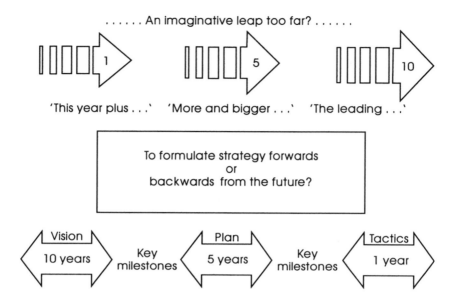

**Figure 14.2** A balanced forwards and backwards view of strategic options is likely to be more reliable than a single direction approach

and expeditionary marketing', to make sure that we view the future uninhibited by today's products and markets relationship. They warn that if the future is seen as an extension of the present it will, in most cases, lead to disaster because competitors can and will get to the same point as well—the competitive ruck will be unprofitable and resource intensive. Central to their thesis on corporate imagination is the need for organizations to drop the products/ markets linkage and think instead of needs and solutions. Only when durable needs are identified and generic solutions evolved is it safe to move to more detailed levels of product specification and market segmentation. I endorse their argument unreservedly provided organizations can be convinced that the only way to adopt the needs/solutions approach is to work to a 10-5-1 strategic framework. I do not think it credible to have forward-looking strategy decoupled from current products and markets thinking: they are simply too attractive as anchors when sailing into future unchartered waters.

Another attraction of the 10-5-1 view is that once the organization has achieved a level of comfort in defining what business to be in, and what it will be like, in 10 years' time through highly facilitated creation of the virtual organization of the twenty-first century, it becomes quite straightforward to look back to the present and define the milestones needed to reach the virtual goal. I generally find that organizations make a good job of the strategic path definition process once they get through the pain barrier of creating their virtual future. The enemy of all strategic thinking is uncertainty. The 10-5-1 approach provides large measures of virtual certainty because it is designed to define fundamentals not details: 'What will people still need in 10 years' time?' is a vastly simpler question than 'What features should this or that product have?'

Similarly, once the future has some clarity to its shape, it becomes relatively easy to assess current assets and capabilities for their suitability for the future of the organization. In the opening chapters of the book I argued that SWOT Analysis undertaken in that logical sequence will lead to tears. The analysis must be OTSW based, so that we only put into our strategic plan the development of assets that will be valuable in seizing the opportunities we see at a profit, and best of all, ahead of the competition. Snapshots of current strengths are, in this view of the world, largely meaningless unless tested with great rigour for their core competence value. Again Hamel and Prahalad have performed a signal service in defining three tests to apply to current strengths. I paraphrase:

- Does each provide wide access to identified current and future opportunities?
- Does each deliver real and significant benefit to clients, in their perception?
- Is each difficult, if not impossible, to imitate?

Of course, all three tests must be satisfied for a current asset or capability to be designated a core competence. However, once these core competences have been identified they take on a radical significance to the business strategist and the marketer in that they represent the prime focus of strategy and management: these are the things that we shall develop and play to. Interestingly, if you find core competences in your organization you should be able to satisfy yourself that they are not vulnerable to short-term environmental problems: rather like a gyro compass they help the organization maintain its attitude regardless of the storms howling outside.

I have stressed this strategic framework point, and especially the 10-5-1 view, since analysis has shown time and again that it is often in the quality of brand management and customer relationship systems

that the real core competences of organizations are to be found.
Take, for example, the *Reader's Digest* organization. I do not think
that their products are their core competence, although some might
argue that the *Reader's Digest* magazine is. Rather, I believe it is their
customer database technologies which allow them to analyse
customer behaviours with incredible sophistication so that the
critical variables that make for the difference between propensity to
buy or not buy are isolated and, in subsequent campaigns,
eliminated. Admittedly, *Reader's Digest* have had 70 years to get the
system right, but they have had no ambiguity for decades about
what they must get right—a system that allows them to understand
why customers do what they do so that they can get them (and
more) to do it again and again. Put another way, *Reader's Digest* are
a business for the twenty-first century, because they are likely to
have exceptional advantages in lifestyle and lifestage analysis
techniques, allowing them to meet the needs of the day, with the
solutions of the day—their competences are their marketing tools
and techniques.

Acceptance of this strategic premise by senior management will
define the things that are valuable, even critical, to long-term
success. If durable opportunities are in view they demand durable
strengths. Durable opportunities attract growing competition.
Therefore, strategy must deliver a competitively bench-marked
growth in core strengths. I believe that there is no more vital
strength to build and play to than quality of relationships with the
key stakeholders in the organization's future—with particular
emphasis on customers and shareholders (in that order).

Now the conditions are improved for a mature debate about the
imperatives of marketing and, especially, the policy framework for
marketing communications. Here I need to return to the myths and
legends and see whether there is a way of integrating the virtues of
this book's arguments with the political realities that you may be
faced with. I believe that marketers need to improve their
accountability and willingness to offer proof of effectiveness. Since
the numerative side of management thinking tends to be viewed
with favour, it is surely good sense to play by those rules. Why so
much of the marketing communications mix should be considered
non-susceptible to numerative analysis defeats me. It is a weakness
that undermines the credibility of the function and its professional
suppliers.

I have no need to argue the case for measurement of telemarketing,
geodemographic systems, electronic systems and direct marketing

as they are all intrinsically measurable. Whether the fact is understood in non-marketing circles is something else.

But other tools and techniques are a numerative challenge: public relations, corporate image, above-the-line advertising, corporate literature and market research all sound useful, but are difficult to prove in purely numerative terms. Hence reading and noting scores, awareness studies, pre- and post-differential analysis, retention, market share and equally malleable measures. Those of you who find the FORENSIC approach attractive will see that it offers a different view of performance effectiveness. Since its whole premise is to be disciplined, structured, even scientific, then it should be helpful in demonstrating to general management and other functions that marketing is not black or white magic, but a process which is fully accountable.

Where many marketers get into difficulties is in their relative inability to explain what each element in the marketing communications mix, being deployed in this or that campaign, is contributing to the whole. I sometimes wonder if marketers know themselves.

Yet this is the critical confidence question. Marketing budgets can be large, the stakes high and the need for accountability real. So why are campaigns designed in such a way that it is difficult to measure the whole effect and, more often than not, impossible to measure the individual contribution of each element? This is less adequate than it might be.

Designing-in measurement is realistic, smart and central to the premise of marketing people being the leaders of learning from experience—the seekers of the better way. While this view may be much more prevalent today in supporting television and large-scale media campaigns, it is almost invisible in below-the-line work outside of direct marketing.

The following checklist should provide a basis for approaching the measurement question.

## How-will-we-know checklist

**14.1**  What customer behaviours are we seeking to change?
**14.2**  What are the current behaviours?
**14.3**  What do we expect the post-facto situation to be?
**14.4**  What can we measure before and after?

**14.5**   What do we need to do to set up the measurement(s)?

**14.6**   What are the easily defined metrics of each communications tool we plan to use?

**14.7**   Which communications tools are the most measurable?

**14.8**   Have we designed-in aspects to the campaign that will increase our facility in measuring change (i.e. response coupons in press advertisements)?

**14.9**   What do we know about the techniques of market research that will help us measure behavioural change?

**14.10** What other functional areas of the organization can provide hard data in support of marketing?

**14.11** What do we have to do to get these data from other functions?

**14.12** What are the fundamental measures of business that are directly linked to marketing activity (even if through other functions such as sales or operations)?

**14.13** How well do we integrate sales performance data with related marketing activity?

**14.14** How well do we use the full range of transactional data held in the accounting systems?

**14.15** How able are we to extrapolate from transactional data information of value to marketing, such as underlying trends, regression analysis, forecasts, comparative time series analysis?

**14.16** What computer resources and skills do we have to provide quality marketing information?

**14.17** How averse are we to making the marketing function numeratively accountable?

**14.18** How well do we design head-to-head tests in our campaigns allowing single variable impact analysis?

**14.19** What are the bench-mark standards in our sector for marketing measurements and who set them?

**14.20** How seriously does our general management want marketing to be numeratively accountable?

**14.21** What responsibility for measurable outcomes do we assign to our suppliers?

**14.22** What use are we making of other data that may be available in the organization and do we know where they are?

**14.23** What are the measurements we need to have to optimize our long-term relationships with each stakeholder?

**14.24** Who in the organization can define success for each stakeholder relationship?

**14.25** What are the standards of performance we should be working to in marketing accountability?

By now it will be apparent that it is a question of mind-set that has the greatest impact on the success or otherwise of marketing accountability. The analytically curious will have little problem with my exhortation to get measuring. They know that there is already a large amount of data available within the organization that can be put to good use: they need only to track it down. One example might serve to make the point. A major commercial lighting company created a state-of-the-art lighting theatre in order to be able to demonstrate every lighting condition, from open-plan offices with large numbers of computer terminals, to the best way to light Granny Smith apples in a supermarket. The aim was to show designers, architects, merchandisers and developers what could be done with the lighting medium. In fact it is a powerful tool for influencing the key decision-makers.

Visitors to the theatre were asked for their business card. Each was given appropriate literature on departure. Few follow-up discussions were arranged. Infrequent checks were made that everyone had, in fact, left a business card. The theatre generated a lot of heat, even with air conditioning, and the remedy of those who suffered was to prop the door open with a shoebox full of the very same business cards—one description of asset management.

This cautionary tale, now well remedied under new management, reminds us that if you do not know the value of your data and their potential uses you are likely to permit the same sort of thing. Again I subscribe to the view that a premium value must be placed upon those in marketing who are curious and seeking to take well-informed decisions rather than upon those who are characterized by originality and flair. Science first, art second: this must also be true of suppliers, whether in isolation or in combination. I warm to suppliers who want to know 'where will this campaign take you and what are we seeking to learn together from it?'

I am not going to open a debate on performance-related pay for marketing suppliers (and marketers themselves), but it might just be worth considering. Certainly the impact on other functions' perceptions of the marketing resource would be profound. The key would be to define the standards and performance measures—the incentive would be clear.

## The ultimate business case for marketing communications

Readers who have reached this point in the book will have had the opportunity to travel through a 360 degree scan of many of the issues in marketing communications and the Forensic approach—whether you are a marketing professional within a client organization, a supplier or a general manager seeking to make sense of the arguments. A number of key themes have been introduced: the need for all marketing activity to be co-ordinated within a strategic framework; the treatment of marketing as primarily a science subject to rigorous analytical techniques; the dangers of assumptiveness; the ability to identify and rationalize the individual and collective merits of the various tools available within marketing communications and, last but not least, the concept that all marketing activity takes place within a series of continua. Marketers must make their optimal impact conscious of the alpha and the omega of their relationships with all the stakeholders of the business.

So what more need be said? One final challenge remains—to establish the business case for investment in the integrated marketing communications plan that is the prime vehicle for delivering Forensic advantage.

Marketing as a function, according to Nigel Piercy of Cardiff Business School, is not universally deemed necessary or valuable. In his authoritative studies (Piercy, 1991) of the issue he has found that significant numbers of organizations have no marketing function *per se*, but rely on everyone to think and behave in a customer-focused way. In other organizations marketing may be an ancillary function to sales, producing materials for their consumption. Yet others have sales reporting to marketing, and, less frequently, every function reporting to marketing! Nigel Piercy analyses the size of department versus its influence and concludes that it is the positioning of the marketing function among the strategic power-brokers of the business that determines its scope and influence.

In those instances where marketing is a comparatively weak function there must be the question of who is taking responsibility for the long view and the full range of relationships with stake-holders that will determine the durable success of the organization? I suspect that these critical marketing issues are neglected in the belief that they belong to the chief executive or company secretary's empire. This seems a short-sighted, high-risk approach.

The business case for the centrality of marketing comes from the
following set of principles for the Forensic Marketing Organization:

1   Marketing is the custodian of all stakeholder relationships.
2   Marketing will be fully accountable for what it does.
3   Suppliers of marketing communications will be valued for their
    ability to realize the aims of the brief they are given.
4   Marketing will brief its suppliers on the business outcomes that
    must be delivered and the measurements that will determine
    success or failure.
5   Marketing will determine a strategic framework for its activities
    that is derived from the business strategy and will explicitly
    relate to the milestones within the strategic plan.
6   Marketing will value a scientific approach that will drive a
    relentless, but structured, search for performance improvement.
7   Marketing will value creativity and entrepreneurship in service
    of activity that will yield explicit and measurable results.
8   Marketing will always seek to validate its assumptions.
9   All functions will recognize the imperative of a co-ordinated
    policy for relationship management.
10  Organizations will encourage and enable the Forensic approach.

These somewhat didactic principles are designed to help marketers
to demonstrate to general management that unity of purpose may
come only through unity of control. The issues that have been
raised in the book and which lie behind the ten principles are too
important for sustainable business advantage to be left
uncoordinated and unallocated in terms of responsibility. If
marketing is about championing the interests of all external
stakeholders within the citadel of the organization then it must be
given the teeth to deliver the right actions. I am sure that any
marketer would accept the awesome accountability that that level of
permission implies. Furthermore, the best suppliers would flock to
work for organizations who place such emphasis on the
management of communications strategy as well as tactical activity
in support of the goals of the moment. Those, too, we cannot
ignore.

# Bibliography and further reading

Ansoff, H.I. (1968) Corporate Strategy, Harmondsworth, Penguin.

Baker, K. and Bermingham, J. (1979) Paper given to the Annual Conference of UK Market Research Society, Brighton.

Bangs, D.H. (1992) *Creating customers*, London, Piatkus.

Beale, R. and Jackson, T. (1994) *Neural computing: an introduction*, Bristol, Institute of Physics Publishing.

Bird, D. (1982) *Commonsense direct marketing*, London, The Printed Shop.

*Business Week* (1993) 'Media mania', *Business Week*, 12 July 1993, pp. 94–101.

*Business Week* (1994) 'The information revolution', *Business Week*, 13 June 1994, pp. 35–59.

Chappell, R.T. and Read, W.L. (1984) *Business communications*, London, Pitman.

Chaston, I. (1993) *Customer-focused marketing*, London, McGraw-Hill.

Chronis, T. (1994) Private paper to a UK national newspaper board of directors.

Collins, A. (1992) *Competitive retail marketing*, London, McGraw-Hill.

Coulson-Thomas, C. (1983) *Marketing communications*, Oxford, Butterworth Heinemann.

Davenport, T.H. (1993) *Process innovation: re-engineering work through information technology*, Cambridge, Mass: Harvard Business School Press.

EDMA/NTC Research (1993) *Direct marketing in Europe: an examination of the statistics*, Marlow, NTC.

Ehrenburg, A. (1988) *Repeat buying*, Oxford, Oxford University Press.

ESOMAR (1993) *European Society for Opinion and Marketing Research Annual Market Study on Market Statistics 1992*, ESOMAR, September.

Fletcher, W. (1990) *Creative people: how to manage them and maximise their creativity*, London, Hutchinson.

Forsyth, P. (1993) *Marketing for non-marketing managers*, London, Pitman.

Hamel, G. and Prahalad, C. K. (1990) 'The core competence of the corporation', *Harvard Business Review*, 1990 (3), pp 79–91.

Hamel, G. and Prahalad, C.K. (1991) Corporate imagination and expeditionary marketing, *Harvard Business Review*, July–August 1991, pp. 81–92.

Hammer, M. and Champy, J.C. (1993) *Re-engineering the corporation*, New York, Harper Business.

Henley Centre (1994) *Teleculture 2000*, The Henley Centre Telebusiness Survey, London, The Henley Centre.

Hutton, P.F. and White, G. (1993) 'Research and the realization of dreams in local government: the case of Colchester Borough Council', AMSO Second Annual Market Research Effectiveness Awards, London, AMSO.

*International Journal of Advertising* (1984).

International Water Supply Association (1992) A talk given by Peter Hutton of MORI to the International Water Supply Association PR workshop, 2 June 1992.

Kosko, B. (1994) *Fuzzy thinking*, London, Harper-Collins.

Latchem, C., Williamson, J. and Henderson-Lancett, L. (eds) (1993) *Interactive multimedia: practices and promises*, London, Kogan Page.

Levitt, T. (1983) *The marketing imagination*, New York, Free Press.

Libfried, K.H.J. and McNair, C.J. (1992) *Benchmarking*, New York, Harper Business.

Llewellyn, D.T. (1985) *Evolution of the British financial system*, London, Institute of Bankers.

Llewellyn, D.T. (1989a) *The banking structure in major countries* (ed) G. G. Kaufman, Federal Reserve Bank of Chicago, USA.

Llewellyn, D.T. (1989b) 'Structural change in the British financial system' in C. Green and D.T. Llewellyn (eds) *Surveys in monetary economics*, vol. 2, Oxford, Blackwell.

McDonald, M.H.B. (1984) *Marketing plans*, Oxford, Heinemann.

McKenna, R. (1992) *Relationship marketing: successful strategies for the age of the customer*, Reading, MA, Addison-Wesley Publishing.

Mitroff, I.I. and Linstone, H.A. (1993) *The unbounded mind*, New York, Oxford University Press.

MORI (1987) *Residents' attitude survey*, August–September 1987. Research study conducted for Solihull Metropolitan Council.

MORI (1988) *Residents' attitude survey*, January–February 1988. Research study conducted by MORI for the London Borough of Richmond-upon-Thames.

Nilson, T.H. (1993) *Value-added marketing*, London, McGraw-Hill.

Peters, T. (1987) *Thriving on chaos*, New York, Knopf.

Piercy, N. (1991) *Market-led strategic change*, London, Thorsons (Harper-Collins).

Porter, M. (1980) *Competitive strategy*, New York, Free Press.

Porter, M. (1985) *Competitive advantage*, New York, Free Press.

Price Waterhouse (1993) *The 1993 market and customer management review*, London, Price Waterhouse.

Printing Industry Research Association (1991) *Ten Year Forecast, 1992–2002*, London, PIRA.

Reichfeld, F. (1993) *Loyalty based management*, a presentation to the Marketing Association Conference, London, Spring 1993, DMA.

Reid, T. (1993) 'They know what you are trying to do', Tim Reid Partnership.

Rheingold, H. (1991) *Virtual reality*, London, Secker & Warburg.

Stewart, R. (1982) *Choices for the manager*

TARP (1988) *800 numbers for customer service, a 1988 profile*, Society of Consumer Affairs Professionals in Business in conjunction with Technical Assistance Research Programmes (TARP), USA.

Toffler, A. (1980) *The third wave*, New York, Bantam.

Wilson, A. (1993) *Marketing audit checklists*, London, McGraw-Hill.

# Index